PRIDE AND PREJUDICE

**A Play with Music
from
Jane Austen's Songbooks**

Written by
Nora Louise Syran
from the novel by Jane Austen

"Without music, life would be a blank to me."

--from Jane Austen's novel *Emma*

Cover image of "The Joys of the Country" courtesy of
Jane Austen's House
Winchester Road, Chawton, Hampshire
GU34 1SD

janeaustens.house

Images throughout the text by Hugh Thompson
Published by George Allen in the 1894 edition of
Pride and Prejudice by Jane Austen

This play was first brought to life in November 2024
by the Accolade Community Theatre of Richardson, TX
under the direction of Desi Brown

The Original Cast and Crew

Mrs. Bennet. Scout Aaron
Elizabeth Bennet. Kendall Arnold
Mr. Bennet. Luke Brown
Mary Bennet. Abby Sowell
Jane Bennet. Jordan Colletti
Kitty Bennet. Dayton Parker
Charles Bingley. Owen Garcia
Fitzwilliam Darcy. Paul Brown
Mrs. Hurst/Elizabeth Bennet Understudy. Ava Villarreal
Caroline Bingley. Lila Houston
Charlotte Lucas. Keeley Stadler
Lydia Bennet. Lily Kenney
Colonel Forster. Micah Peek
Mrs. Forster. Mary Cross
Sir William Lucas/Servant. Quinn McClure
Lady Lucas/Mrs. Hill/Mary King. Elise Bobadilla
Mr. Collins. Cole Fletcher
Mr. Wickham. Kai Stadler
Mr. Phillips. David Helm
Mrs. Phillips/Mrs. Younge. Isabella Turner
Mrs. Gardiner. Emma Dooley
Mr. Gardiner. Joshua Brown
Lady Catherine de Bourgh. Nora Mano
Anne de Bourgh/Kitty Bennet Understudy. Katelyn Polsky
Colonel Fitzwilliam. Samuel Sowell
Georgiana Darcy. Julia Lopez
Mrs. Reynolds/Mrs. Hurst. Understudy. Adelay Spencer
Mr. Denny. Sam Peek
Ensemble. Bella Brown
Ensemble/Jane and Mary Understudy. Cara Deatherage
Ensemble/Lydia Bennet Understudy. Grace Bell
Ensemble/Mr. Collins Understudy. Mace Winkler
Crew. Carissa Bergsagel, Charlotte Valentine, Elise Garcia, Ella
Bates, Hixson Mano, Zachary Nicholson
Tech. Andrew Bell, Mitchell Isaak

CAST OF CHARACTERS
20F + 11M + ENSEMBLE

(M/F) Ensemble of officers, servants of Longbourn, Netherfield, Rosings and Lambton Inn and villagers of Meryton and guests of the Assembly and Netherfield balls.

(F) Elizabeth (Eliza, Lizzy) Bennet (20) An intelligent young woman who possesses a keen wit.

(F) Jane Bennet (22) The eldest. Gentle and kind-hearted.

(F) Mrs. Bennet (40) Elizabeth's melodramatic mother.

(F) Lydia Bennet (15-16) The irresponsible youngest sister.

(F) Catherine (Kitty) Bennet (17) The petulant sister.

(F) Mary Bennet (18) The pedantic Bennet sister.

(F) Charlotte Lucas (27) Lizzy's closest friend; sensible.

(F) Caroline Bingley (20) Mr. Bingley's shallow sister.

(F) Mrs. Hurst (22) Mr. Bingley's gossiping sister.

(F) Mrs. Reynolds (40) Mr. Darcy's devoted Housekeeper.

(F) Mrs. Younge (40) + Georgiana Darcy's governess.

(F) Lady Lucas (45) + Sir William's charming wife.

(F) Mrs. Phillips (40) + Mrs. Bennet's coarse sister.

(F) Mrs. Gardiner (30) Mrs. Bennet's perceptive sister-in-law.

(F) Lady Catherine De Bourgh (50) Mr. Darcy's aunt.

(F) Mrs. Forster (18) + Colonel Forster's young, joyful wife.

(F) Mary King (18) + A near-conquest of Mr. Wickham's.

(F) Mrs. Hill (50) * Ever patient housekeeper of Longbourn.

(F) Georgiana Darcy (16) Mr. Darcy's timid sister.

(F) Miss Anne de Burgh (28) + Lady Catherine's daughter.

(M) Mr. Bennet (50) Elizabeth's droll and discontented father.

(M) Fitzwilliam Darcy (28) A wealthy, proud and private man.

(M) George Wickham (27) A man who hides a dark, manipulative side behind his good looks and happy manners.

(M) Charles Bingley (23) Mr. Darcy's good-natured friend.

(M) **Mr. Collins (25)** Mr. Bennet's silly obsequious cousin.
(M) **Sir William Lucas (50)** Charlotte's good natured father.
(M) **Mr. Gardiner (40)** Mrs. Bennet's well-mannered brother.
(M) **Colonel Fitzwilliam (25)** Mr. Darcy's cousin.
(M) **Colonel Forster (30)** * A sensible man.
(M) **Mr. Denny (25)** + An officer, friend to Mr. Wickham.
(M) **Mr. Phillips (50)** + A stuffy attorney. Uncle to the girls.
+ *non speaking * one line*

SUGGESTED CASTING FOR AN ENSEMBLE OF 18

F1. Elizabeth (Eliza, Lizzy) Bennet
F2. Jane Bennet
F3. Mrs. Bennet
F4. Lydia Bennet
F5. Catherine (Kitty) Bennet; Anne de Bourgh
F6. Mary Bennet
F7. Charlotte Lucas (27)
F8. Caroline Bingley (20)
F9. Mrs. Hurst; Mrs. Reynolds; Mrs. Younge
F10. Mrs. Hill; Lady Lucas; Mrs. Phillips; Mrs. Gardiner; Lady
Catherine De Bourgh
F11. Mrs. Forster; Mary King; Georgiana Darcy
M1. Mr. Bennet
M2. Fitzwilliam Darcy
M3. George Wickham
M4. Charles Bingley
M5. Mr. Collins, Mr. Denny, an officer (25)
M6. Sir William Lucas; Mr. Phillips, Mr. Gardiner
M7. Colonel Forster; Colonel Fitzwilliam

A NOTE REGARDING THE MUSIC

This play includes music from Jane Austen's own songbooks. While we don't know all the songs she "practiced regularly every morning," as her niece Caroline wrote, we know "she played very pretty tunes...much that she played from was manuscript, copied out by herself—and so neatly and correctly, that it was as easy to read as print." Some of the songs in this show are written out in her own hand, like "The Joys of the Country" and some are from printed sheets by composers we know she enjoyed. We know that "Robin Adair," for example, was a particular favorite of hers. We also know Scottish and Irish airs were very popular in her day which is why I've included Robert Burns' "Their Groves of Sweet Myrtle" from the family books and have taken poetic license with her contemporary Beethoven's "What Shall I do to Show How Much I Love Her?" and some other traditional tunes of her time. Contact me for more information, the sheet music and additional music and production notes. www.sagascripts.com

THE JOYS OF THE COUNTRY Charles Dibdin
SOUND ARGUMENT Charles Dibdin
HOW SWEET IN THE WOODLANDS Henry Harington
ROBIN ADAIR (traditional)
HOW MISTAKEN IS THE LOVER Stephen Storace
GREENSLEEVES traditional)
DRIVE THE COLD WINTER AWAY (traditional)
THEIR GROVES OF SWEET MYRTLE Robert Burns
THO YOU THINK BY THIS TO VEX ME Stephen Storace
I ATTEMPT FROM LOVE'S SICKNESS Henry Purcell
WHAT SHALL I DO TO SHOW HOW MUCH I LOVE HER? Beethoven
I HAVE A SILENT SORROW HERE Georgiana Spencer Cavendish
BEGONE DULL CARE (traditional)

NOTES REGARDING STAGING

The set design may be as minimal or as extravagant as needed as long as it allows for the music, movement and dialogue to punctuate the transitions of the scenes as they blend fluidly from one to the next.

While it is possible to perform this play with a cast of 18, a solid group of additional singers/dancers to play the non speaking roles, servants, gardeners, soldiers, ball guests etc is highly recommended. Stage crew costumed as servants is an effective way of assuring smooth transitions between scenes.

It is recommended you remain as true to the spirit of Austen's novel as possible as far as staging and music, but in regard to casting, actors can be any race/ethnicity.

Ages of the characters in the novel are noted but need not be strictly adhered to except in the age range of the sisters.

ACT ONE

Prologue. The Countryside & Bennet Family home, Longbourn
—THE JOYS OF THE COUNTRY

Scene 1. October. Longbourn

Scene 2. A fortnight later at the Assembly Ball and Longbourn
—THE JOYS OF THE COUNTRY (reprise)

Scene 3. A fortnight later at the Home of the Sir William and Lady Lucas
—SOUND ARGUMENT

Scene 4. November at Longbourn
— THE JOYS OF THE COUNTRY (reprise)

Scene 5. The next morning walking to Meryton and Netherfield
— THE JOYS OF THE COUNTRY (reprise)

Scene 6. Some hours later in the drawing room of Netherfield

Scene 7. That evening in the drawing room of Netherfield

Scene 8. Moments later in the drawing room of Netherfield
— HOW SWEET IN THE WOODLANDS

Scene 9. The following morning. Drawing room of Netherfield

Scene 10. That evening. Drawing room of Netherfield
—HOW SWEET IN THE WOODLANDS (reprise)

Scene 11. Leaving to return home to Longbourn
—HOW SWEET IN THE WOODLANDS (reprise)

Scene 12. Walking to Meryton.
—HOW SWEET IN THE WOODLANDS (reprise)

Scene 13. The following evening at the Phillips home.

Scene 14. Returning home to Longbourn later that evening.

Scene 15. The following week. The ballroom at Netherfield
— ROBIN ADAIR

Scene 16. The following morning at Longbourn
—HOW MISTAKEN IS THE LOVER

Scene 17. Moments later at Longbourn.

Scene 18. December. The church at Meryton
— HOW MISTAKEN IS THE LOVER (reprise)

Scene 19. Approaching Christmas at Longbourn
— GREENSLEEVES & DRIVE THE COLD WINTER AWAY

Scene 3. July at Pemberley. The house and the grounds
—I ATTEMPT FROM LOVE'S SICKNESS TO FLY

Scene 4. The Inn at Lambton the following morning
—WHAT SHALL I DO TO SHOW HOW MUCH I LOVE HER?

Scene 5. August at the Inn at Lambton
—WHAT SHALL I DO TO SHOW HOW MUCH I LOVE HER? (Reprise)

Scene 6. The Inn at Lambton. Longbourn and London.

Scene 7. Later in August. Longbourn.

Scene 8. September. The village of Meryton and Longbourn.

Scene 9. A week later. Longbourn
—I HAVE A SILENT SORROW HERE
—THE JOYS OF THE COUNTRY (reprise)

Scene 10. October at Longbourn
—HOW SWEET IN THE WOODLANDS (Reprise)
—THOU YOU THINK BY THIS TO VEX ME (reprise)

Scene 11. Leaving Longbourn to walk to Oakham Mount.

Scene 12. Not long after. Longbourn.

Scene 13. November at Pemberley.

EPILOGUE — BEGONE DULL CARE

ACT ONE

PROLOGUE

*T*he ENSEMBLE introduces the characters and key elements of the plot by singing THE JOYS OF THE COUNTRY by Charles Dibdin. CAROLINE BINGLEY and MRS. HURST are removed from the jolly company, as is MR. DARCY who, while shooting with his friend MR. BINGLEY —who is charmed by the countryside — is seemingly cold and distant. LYDIA flirts with the OFFICERS. MR. WICKHAM is drawn to ELIZABETH BENNET who follows behind the others, observant. She chats occasionally with her friend CHARLOTTE LUCAS. JANE gathers flowers on the walk. MR. COLLINS looks on, adoringly.*

ENSEMBLE.

> LET BUCKS AND LET BLOODS
> TO PRAISE LONDON AGREE
> OH, THE JOYS OF THE COUNTRY
> MY JEWEL, FOR ME

Longbourn, the Bennet family home. MR. BENNET and MRS. BENNET enter, both with letters. The ENSEMBLE scene and the Longbourn scene happen simultaneously.

MRS. BENNET. Mr. Bennet! Mr. Bennet?

(The Ensemble picks up singing and stage business in between the dialogue.)
ENSEMBLE.
> WHERE SWEET IS THE FLOW'R
> THAT THE MAY-BUSH ADORNS
> AND HOW CHARMING TO GATHER IT

ELIZABETH. *(Underscoring the irony.)*
> BUT FOR THE THORNS

MRS. BENNET. Netherfield is to be let at last! Do you not want to know who has taken it?

MR. BENNET. You want to tell me, and I have no objection to hearing it.

(Mr. Bingley stands with fishing rod in hand, happy in the countryside.)

MRS. BENNET. Netherfield has been taken by a young man of large fortune by the name of Bingley, and he is single, my dear. Think of that, Mr. Bennet! What a fine thing for our girls!

MR. BENNET. Our girls? How so? How can it affect them?

MRS. BENNET. Oh, Mr. Bennet, you must know that I am thinking of his marrying one of them but it will be impossible for us to visit him if you do not.

MR. BENNET. You and the girls may go. I dare say Mr. Bingley will be very glad to see you and he might like you the best of the party, my dear.

MRS BENNET. *(Charmed, coquettish)* Oh, Mr. Bennet!

MR BENNET. But I must throw in a good word for my little Lizzy.

MRS. BENNET. I desire you will do no such thing! Lizzy is not half as handsome as Jane… *(Jane avoids Mr. Collins while Elizabeth walks with Mr. Wickham.)* Nor as good-humoured as Lydia. *(Lydia giggles with the soldiers.)* But you are always giving Lizzy the preference. *(Charlotte Lucas stands and listens to Mr. Collins.)*

MR. BENNET. They are all silly and ignorant girls; but Lizzy has something more of quickness than her sisters.

ENSEMBLE.
>WHERE WE WALK O'ER THE MOUNTAINS
>WITH HEALTH OUR CHEEKS GLOWING

MEN OF THE ENSEMBLE.
>AS WARM AS A TOAST, HONEY

WOMEN OF THE ENSEMBLE.
>WHEN IT AIN'T SNOWING!

MRS. BENNET. It is very likely that Mr. Bingley will fall in love with one of them, and therefore you must visit him as soon as you can!

ENSEMBLE.
>WHERE NATURE TO SMILE
>WHEN SHE JOYFUL INCLINES
>AND THE SUN CHARMS US
>ALL THE YEAR ROUND

ELIZABETH BENNETT.
>WHEN IT SHINES

(Thunder. A storm is coming. Mary, who has not been walking, enters.)

MRS. BENNET. We shall never know Mr. Bingley nor his excellent sisters!

Oh, Mr. Bennet, you have no compassion on my poor nerves.

MR. BENNET. You mistake, my dear. I have a high respect for your nerves. They've been my old friends these twenty years at least.

ENSEMBLE.

> OH, THE MOUNTAINS AND VALLEYS
> AND BUSHES
> THE PIGS AND THE SCREECH-OWLS
> AND THRUSHES
> LET BUCKS AND LET BLOODS
> TO PRAISE LONDON AGREE
> OH, THE JOYS OF THE COUNTRY,
> MY JEWEL, FOR ME

MR. BENNET. My dear, we are to expect my cousin, Mr. Collins, who, when I am dead, may turn you all out of this house as soon as he pleases.

MRS. BENNET. Oh! My dear! Pray do not talk of that odious man.

(Mr. Collins ogles at Jane. Mary studies the letter from Mr. Collins.)

MR. BENNET. While nothing can clear Mr. Collins from the guilt of inheriting Longbourn, he *(citing the letter)* "comes prepared to admire" our daughters which I assume he means to/

MRS. BENNET. *(Suddenly appreciative of Mr. Collins)* Marry one of them!

MARY. The idea of the olive-branch perhaps is not wholly new, yet I think it is well expressed/ *(Mr. Collins approaches Jane Bennet once again.)*

MRS. BENNET. Yes, yes Mary… *(Mr. Darcy stands aiming a rifle while Mr. Bingley is fishing. The Bingley Sisters are bored and shivering in the cold.)*

MEN OF THE ENSEMBLE.
> THERE TWELVE HOURS ON A STRETCH
> WE IN ANGLING DELIGHT
> AS PATIENT AS JOBS
> THOUGH WE GET NE'ER A BITE
> THERE WE POP AT THE WILD DUCKS
> AND FRIGHTEN THE CROWS

(Mr. Darcy shoots. The ladies cover their ears and shiver.)

WOMEN OF THE ENSEMBLE.
> WHILE SO LIVELY THE ICICLES
> HANG TO OUR CLOTHES

MRS. BENNET. I am sick of Mr. Bingley and the talk of his fine sisters...

MR. BENNET. I am sorry to hear that. If I had known, I certainly should not have called upon him.

MRS. BENNET. Oh, my dear Mr. Bennet! I was sure you loved your girls too well to neglect such an acquaintance! If I can but see one of my daughters happily settled at Netherfield and all the others equally well married, I shall have nothing to wish for. *(Mrs. Bennet hurries off in delight. Mary exits, studying the letter. Mr. Bennet retreats to the quiet of his library. Lydia steps between Mr. Wickham and Elizabeth.)*

WOMEN OF THE ENSEMBLE.
> THERE WITH AUNTS AND WILD COUSINS
> AND GRANDMOTHERS TALKING
> WE'RE CAUGHT IN THE RAIN
> AS WE'RE ALL OUT A-WALKING

MEN OF THE ENSEMBLE.
> WHILE THE MUSLINS AND GAUZES
> CLING ROUND EACH FAIR SHE
> SO THEY LOOK ALL LIKE VENUSES
> SPRUNG FROM THE SEA.

(Troubled, Mr. Darcy watches Mr. Wickham.)

ENSEMBLE.
> OH, THE MOUNTAINS AND VALLEYS
> AND BUSHES,
> THE PIGS AND THE SCREECH-OWLS
> AND THRUSHES
> LET BUCKS AND LET BLOODS
> TO PRAISE LONDON AGREE
> OH, THE JOYS OF THE COUNTRY,
> MY JEWEL, FOR ME *(repeat)*

(The Ensemble gathers in tableaux and the couples join together as in the conclusion of the story: Jane and Mr. Bingley, Lydia and Mr. Wickham, Mr. Collins and Charlotte. All watch as Elizabeth and Mr. Darcy observe each other for the first time.)

ELIZABETH. *(To the audience)* It is a truth universally acknowledged, that a single man in possession of a good fortune, must be in want of a wife.

(The spell is broken as Lydia shrieks with laughter as the sisters return home to Longbourn.)

SCENE ONE

JANE. Really, mamma, you must speak to Lydia

MRS. BENNET. Nonsense! She has high animal spirits. Oh, Jane, Lizzy, Lydia! Your father has received a visit from Mr. Bingley!

ELIZABETH. Kitty? Mary?

MARY. All we could see from the upper window is that he wore a blue coat/

KITTY. ...and rode a black horse. And we heard him say he has returned with a party for the assembly ball!

MARY. Five altogether: Mr. Bingley, his two sisters, the husband of the eldest, and another young man, very proud they say...a/

SCENE TWO

Elizabeth announces Mr. Darcy's entrance as the Ensemble sings and forms lines for the assembly ball.

ELIZABETH. ...Mr. Darcy

ENSEMBLE.
OH THE MOUNTAINS AND VALLEYS
AND BUSHES,
THE PIGS AND THE SCREECH OWLS
AND THRUSHES!
LET BUCKS AND LET BLOODS
TO PRAISE LONDON AGREE,
OH, THE JOYS OF THE COUNTRY,

MY JEWEL FOR ME! *(repeat)*
(The ensemble dance. At least four couples are formed. Bingley is charmed by all he sees. The dance and the conversation at Longbourn happen simultaneously with Mrs. Bennet narrating the events of the evening prior.)

MRS. BENNET. Oh, my dear Mr. Bennet, we have had a most delightful evening, a most excellent ball. Lydia was never without partners! *(Lydia, laughing, flirts with an office at the assembly ball. Mary and Kitty enter Longbourn undoing their bonnets. Mr. Bingley finishes a dance with Charlotte Lucas, sees Jane dance with an officer, asks to be introduced and it is love at first sight as in the Prologue. They appear to be dancing alone in an empty ballroom.)*

MARY. I heard someone tell Miss Bingley that I'm the most accomplished girl in the neighbourhood.

MRS. BENNET. Yes, yes Mary... Jane was so admired.

KITTY. Mr. Bingley danced with her twice!

MARY. He danced first with Miss Lucas/

MRS. BENNET. But he seemed quite struck with Jane, so he got introduced, and asked her to dance!

MARY. Then danced with his sister Mrs. Hurst/

KITTY. ...and then with his other sister Caroline Bingley/

MARY. And then Jane, again!

MR. BENNET. For God's sake, say no more of his partners. Oh, that he had sprained his ankle in the first dance! What of Lizzy?

(Mr. Darcy stands apart from everyone. Mr. Bingley notices this and reluctantly leaves Jane to speak with him

while she then talks with Caroline Bingley and Mrs. Hurst. Elizabeth sits and overhears Mr. Darcy and Mr. Bingley.)

MRS. BENNET. Lizzy was obliged, by the scarcity of gentlemen and the refusal of Mr. Darcy to dance, to sit down for two dances. He walked here, and he walked there, fancying himself so very great! I quite detest the man.

MR. BINGLEY. Come, Darcy, I must have you dance. I hate to see you standing about by yourself in this stupid manner.

MR. DARCY. I certainly shall not. You know how I detest it, unless I am particularly acquainted with my partner. Your sisters are engaged, and there is not another woman in the room whom it would not be a punishment to me to stand up with.

MR. BINGLEY. Upon my honour, I never met with so many pleasant girls in my life as I have this evening; and there are several of them you see uncommonly pretty.

MR. DARCY. You are dancing with the only handsome girl in the room.

MR. BINGLEY. Oh! She is the most beautiful creature I ever beheld! But there is one of her sisters sitting down just behind you, who is very pretty indeed. Do let me ask my partner to introduce you.

MR. DARCY. Which do you mean? *(Turns to see Elizabeth.)* She is tolerable, I suppose; but not handsome enough to tempt me/

(Elizabeth takes over recounting Mr. Darcy's words, their voices blending; she is amused and laughs, joins her friend Charlotte, yet her pride has been wounded.)

MR. DARCY/ELIZABETH. (*Voices overlapping*) ...and I am in no humour at present to give consequence to young ladies who are slighted by other men.

MR. BENNET. My Lizzy? Slighted? By Mr. Darcy?

ENSEMBLE. (*Lines divided, some spoken separately, some in unison.*) He has ten thousand a year! Mr. Darcy declined being introduced to any other lady in the room. He is the proudest, most disagreeable man in the world. What a contrast between him and his friend, Mr. Bingley. We are to dine in a fortnight with the Lucas's and I very much hope Mr. Darcy will not be invited. So very proud. (*Jane and Lizzy talk privately.*)

JANE. Mr. Bingley is just what a young man ought to be. Sensible, good-humoured, lively/

ELIZABETH. And handsome...

JANE. Yes! I was very much flattered by his asking me to dance a second time.

ELIZABETH. He could not help seeing that you were about five times as pretty as every other woman in the room. (*pause*) And so, you like this man's sisters, too, do you?

JANE. Certainly not; at first. But I am much mistaken, Lizzy, if we shall not find them very charming neighbours. (*Sighs*) We will meet them again very soon at the Lucas's/

SCENE THREE

The following scene flows on from the last as Sir Lucas, Lady Lucas and Charlotte Lucas greet the Bingley party.

Jane "announces" their entrance as she and Elizabeth observe them arrive. The Bingley sisters, Caroline and Mrs. Hurst, gossip together as they enter. Mr. Bingley and Mr. Darcy follow behind.)

JANE. …Mrs. Hurst.
MRS. HURST. *(To Caroline Bingley)* Mrs. Bennet is intolerable and the younger sisters not worth knowing/
JANE. Caroline Bingley.
CAROLINE BINGLEY. But we agree, sister: we do wish to be better acquainted with the eldest Miss Jane Bennet.
(Mrs. Bennet and Elizabeth then talk with Charlotte Lucas while Mr. Darcy looks on. Jane and Mr. Bingley are very happy in each other's company; all notice.)
MRS. BENNET. You began the last assembly ball well, Charlotte. You were Mr. Bingley's first choice.
CHARLOTTE LUCAS. Yes; but he seemed to like his second better. *(They look at Mr. Bingley and Mr. Darcy as they pass by.)* Poor Eliza! To be only just tolerable.
MRS. BENNET. Another time, Lizzy - but I would not dance with him, if I were you.
ELIZABETH BENNET. I believe, ma'am, I may safely promise you never to dance with him.
CHARLOTTE LUCAS. So very fine a young man, with family, fortune; he has a right to be proud..?
ELIZABETH. *(to the audience)* I could easily forgive his pride, if he had not mortified mine.
MARY. Human nature is particularly prone to pride. But a person may be proud without being vain. Pride relates

more to our opinion of ourselves, vanity to what we would *have* others think of us.

MRS. BENNET. Yes, yes Mary...

CHARLOTTE LUCAS. Mr. Bingley likes your sister undoubtedly; but he may never do more than like her, if she does not help him on.

ELIZABETH. But she is not acting by design. She has known him only a fortnight. This is not quite long enough to make her understand his character.

CHARLOTTE LUCAS. Well, I wish Jane success with all my heart. Happiness in marriage is entirely a matter of chance. It is better to know as little as possible of the defects of the person with whom you are to pass your life.

ELIZABETH. You make me laugh, Charlotte; you would never act in this way yourself!? *(Lydia interrupts Lizzy and pulls her toward the officers.)*

LYDIA. Lizzy, you promised....!

ELIZABETH. Colonel Forster! My sister Lydia entreats me to ask if you will be hosting a ball in Meryton while you are headquartered here? *(To the audience)* Lydia and Kitty can talk of nothing but officers.

COLONEL FORSTER. Mrs. Forster is exceedingly fond of dancing, isn't that so my dear?

MRS. FORSTER. We would be delighted! Now then Lydia...

(Lydia emits a loud squeal and she and the young Mrs. Forster walk off together, chatting. Kitty follows behind. Elizabeth notices that Mr. Darcy has been moving slowly closer to her. Elizabeth and Charlotte chat quietly with Colonel Forster.)

ELIZABETH. *(To Charlotte)* What does Mr. Darcy mean by listening to my conversation with Colonel Forster? *(To the audience)* If I do not begin by being impertinent myself, I shall soon grow afraid of him.

CHARLOTTE LUCAS. *(Teasingly.)* It will be her turn soon to be teased, Mr. Darcy! I am going to open the instrument, Eliza, you know what follows!

ELIZABETH. You are always wanting me to play and sing before anybody and everybody! I would really rather not sit down before those who are in the habit of hearing the very best performers. *(Charlotte persists, pulls her to the piano.)* Very well…

SIR WILLIAM LUCAS. *(Joining his sullen guest, Mr. Darcy.)* You are adept in the science of the dance yourself, Mr. Darcy?

(Mr. Darcy is pulled into conversation but he would rather observe Elizabeth Bennet.)

MR. DARCY. It is a compliment I never pay to any place if I can avoid it.

(Elizabeth sits at the instrument and begins to play SOUND ARGUMENT by Charles Dibdin. Most listen, some talk, some dance.)

MRS. BENNET. *(Warning her.)* Lizzy, remember where you are!

ELIZABETH.

    WE BIPEDS, MADE UP OF FRAIL CLAY

MRS. BENNET. Oh, Lizzy!

ELIZABETH.

    ALAS! ARE THE CHILDREN OF SORROW
    AND THOUGH BRISK AND MERRY TO-DAY

WE ALL MAY BE WRETCHED TO-MORROW

SIR WILLIAM LUCAS. Your friend performs delightfully.

ELIZABETH.

FOR SUNSHINE'S SUCCEEDED BY RAIN
THEN, FEARFUL OF LIFE'S
STORMY WEATHER
LEST PLEASURE SHOULD ONLY BRING PAIN
LET US ALL BE UNHAPPY TOGETHER
LET US ALL BE UNHAPPY TOGETHER
LET US ALL BE UNHAPPY TOGETHER

FOR SUNSHINE'S
SUCCEEDED   BY RAIN
THEN, FEARFUL OF LIFE'S
STORMY WEATHER
LEST PLEASURE SHOULD
ONLY BRING PAIN
LET US ALL BE UNHAPPY
TOGETHER

IF A MORTAL WOULD POINT OUT THAT LIFE
WHICH ON EARTH COULD BE
NEAREST TO HEAVEN,
LET HIM, THANKING HIS STARS,
CHOOSE A WIFE
TO WHOM TRUTH AND HONOUR ARE GIVEN

BUT HONOUR AND TRUTH ARE SO RARE
AND HORNS, WHEN THEY'RE CUTTING

SO TINGLE

THAT WILL ALL MY RESPECT FOR THE FAIR

I'D ADVISE HIM TO SIGH AND LIVE SINGLE

I'D ADVISE HIM TO SIGH AND LIVE SINGLE

I'D ADVISE HIM TO SIGH AND LIVE SINGLE

ELIZABETH. *(Elizabeth looks directly at Mr. Darcy.)*

AND WITH ALL MY RESPECT FOR THE FAIR,

I'D ADVISE HIM TO SIGH AND LIVE SINGLE.

(Some women giggle and some applaud politely. The Bingley sisters are shocked. Elizabeth returns to Charlotte, passing by the two men.)

SIR WILLIAM LUCAS. Mr. Darcy, you must allow me to present this young lady to you as a very desirable partner. *(Sir William takes Elizabeth's hand to give to Mr. Darcy but she instantly draws it back.)*

ELIZABETH. Indeed, sir, I have not the least intention of dancing. I entreat you not to suppose that I moved this way in order to beg for a partner.

MR. DARCY. May I have the honour, Miss Bennet?

ELIZABETH. Mr. Darcy is all politeness...

SIR WILLIAM LUCAS. He is, indeed—but, who would object to such a partner?

ELIZABETH. *(archly to audience)* Who indeed?

(She turns away from Mr. Darcy. He watches her go. Caroline Bingley joins Mr. Darcy. As they talk, the scene returns to Longbourn.)

CAROLINE BINGLEY. I can guess the subject of your reverie.

MR. DARCY. I should imagine not.

CAROLINE BINGLEY. You are considering how insupportable it would be to pass many evenings in this manner — in such society.

MR. DARCY. No. My mind was more agreeably engaged. I have been meditating on the very great pleasure which a pair of fine eyes in the face of a pretty woman can bestow.

CAROLINE BINGLEY. And what lady has inspired such reflections, Mr. Darcy?

MR. DARCY. Miss Elizabeth Bennet.

CAROLINE BINGLEY. Miss Elizabeth Bennet! I am all astonishment. Pray when am I to wish you joy?

MR. DARCY. A lady's imagination is very rapid; it jumps from admiration to love, from love to matrimony, in a moment.

CAROLINE BINGLEY. I consider the matter as absolutely settled. And with you always at Pemberley, you will have a charming mother-in-law, indeed…

SCENE FOUR

At Longbourn. Jane has read a letter to her mother who shrieks with joy.

MRS. BENNET. An invitation to dine with Miss Bingley!? Oh! No you may not have the carriage! You had better go on horseback,

because it seems likely to rain; and then you must stay all night! *(They wave goodbye to Jane. Thunder rumbles in the distance. Sound of rain.)* This was a lucky idea of mine, indeed!

ELIZABETH. *(To the audience)* As if the credit of making it rain were all her own.
(Speak-sings to herself, full of worry.)
>   CAUGHT IN THE RAIN *(sighs)*
>   AS SHE'S OUT A-WALKING
>   *(Hopefully)* SHE'LL LOOK LIKE A VENUS
>   WHO'S SPRUNG FROM THE SEA

(The next morning. Elizabeth is pacing. A servant from Netherfield brings a note.)

ELIZABETH. Jane is ill! I will go to her. *(Observing the clear sky.)* I shall walk.

MRS. BENNET. Walk? To Netherfield in all that dirt!? You will not be fit to be seen when you get there.

ELIZABETH. I shall be very fit to see Jane — which is all I want. It's only three miles. I shall be back by dinner.

KITTY. We will go as far as Meryton with you!

LYDIA. If we make haste perhaps we may see something of Captain Carter before he goes!?

SCENE FIVE

They walk to Meryton/Netherfield. During the course of the song, Elizabeth separates from her sisters, enters the front hall of Netherfield, the bottom of her dress is covered in mud. Mr. Darcy and Mr. Bingley greet her. The Bingley sisters, Caroline Bingley and Mrs. Hurst, look her over from head to toe. Elizabeth inquires about her sister, Jane, and exits with the Housekeeper to see her.

ENSEMBLE.
> OH, THE MOUNTAINS AND VALLEYS
> AND BUSHES,
> THE PIGS AND THE SCREECH-OWLS
> AND THRUSHES
> LET BUCKS AND LET BLOODS
> TO PRAISE LONDON AGREE,
> OH, THE JOYS OF THE COUNTRY,
> MY JEWEL, FOR ME *(Repeat)*

CAROLINE BINGLEY. To walk three miles, or whatever it is, above her ankles in dirt, and alone, quite alone! It seems to me to show an abominable sort of conceited independence!

MR. BINGLEY. It shows an affection for her sister that is very pleasing.

MRS. HURST. I hope you saw her petticoat, six inches deep in mud, I am absolutely certain.

MR. BINGLEY. I thought Miss Elizabeth Bennet looked remarkably well. Her dirty petticoat quite escaped my notice.

CAROLINE BINGLEY. You observed it, Mr. Darcy, I am sure. And I am inclined to think that you would not wish to see your sister make such an exhibition.

MR. DARCY. *(Looking after where Lizzy has exited. Wistfully.)* Certainly not.

SCENE SIX

Elizabeth returns to the Bingleys and Mr. Darcy.

CAROLINE BINGLEY. How does your sister, Miss Bennet?

ELIZABETH. I thank you. Jane is by no means better, I'm afraid. But the Doctor has come and gone. With your permission I'll return in the morning.

MRS. HURST. I do so dislike being ill. Oh, poor Jane. Well, she must stay as long as she likes. *(To her sister for approval).* As I suppose must you, Miss Bennet.

CAROLINE BINGLEY. We'll send a servant to Longbourn to acquaint the family with your stay... *(Looking at Elizabeth's dress and petticoat, the hem covered in mud.)* and bring back a supply of clothes. Dinner is at half-past six. *(Elizabeth exits to change for dinner. Simultaneously, at Longbourn, the Bennets prepare a small trunk to send off with a servant.)*

MR. BENNET. Well, my dear, if your daughter should die, it would be a comfort to know that it was all in pursuit of Mr. Bingley, and under your orders.

MRS. BENNET. Oh! People do not die of little trifling colds. She will be taken good care of. As long as she stays there, it is all very well.

(The scene returns to Netherfield where the Bennet sisters are gossiping.)

CAROLINE BINGLEY. Miss Jane Bennet is really a very sweet girl.

MRS. HURST. But Miss Elizabeth Bennet has nothing to recommend her, but being an excellent walker!

CAROLINE BINGLEY. Yes! But with an uncle who is an attorney in Meryton and another who lives somewhere near Cheapside! *(They both laugh heartily.)*
MR. BINGLEY. If they had uncles enough to fill all Cheapside, it would not make them one jot less agreeable.
MR. DARCY. *(Matter of factly, seriously but without malice.)* But it must very materially lessen their chance of marrying men of any consideration in the world.
MRS. HURST. Indeed. Now, Miss Elizabeth Bennet. I shall never forget her appearance this morning. She really looked almost wild.
CAROLINE BINGLEY. Scampering about the country, because her sister had a cold? I am afraid, Mr. Darcy that this adventure has rather affected your admiration of her fine eyes.
MR. DARCY. Not at all; they were brightened by the exercise.

SCENE SEVEN

Evening at Netherfield. Mr. Bingley and his sisters sit to play cards. Mr. Darcy writes a letter. Elizabeth Bennet enters, sits apart from them and reads.

MRS. HURST. Do you prefer reading to cards, Miss Elizabeth? That is rather singular.
CAROLINE BINGELY. Miss Eliza Bennet despises cards. She is a great reader, and has no pleasure in anything else.

ELIZABETH. I deserve neither such praise nor such censure. I am not a great reader, and I have pleasure in many things.

MR. BINGLEY. In nursing your sister I am sure you have pleasure and I hope it will soon be increased by seeing her quite well.

ELIZABETH. I thank you, sir.

CAROLINE BINGLEY. I regret we've such a small collection of books for you to choose from, Miss Bennet. *(Coyly.)* What a delightful library you have at Pemberley, Mr. Darcy!

MR. DARCY. *(Not looking up.)* It ought to be good, it has been the work of many generations.

MR. BINGLEY. And then you have added so much to it yourself. You are always buying books.

CAROLINE BINGLEY. Oh, Pemberley. There is not a finer county in England than Derbyshire nor a finer house than Pemberely. How delighted Miss Darcy will be to receive such a long letter! *(He does not reply.)* Pray tell

your sister that I long to see her. *(Elizabeth puts down her book and draws near the card-table to observe the game. She stands. Mr. Darcy looks up. Watches her.)*

MR. DARCY. *(To Caroline.)* I have already told her so once, by your desire.

CAROLINE BINGLEY. Is Miss Darcy much grown since the spring?

MR. DARCY. She is now about... Miss Elizabeth Bennet's height, perhaps taller.

CAROLINE BINGLEY. So extremely accomplished for her age! Her performance on the pianoforte is exquisite.

MR. BINGLEY. It is amazing to me how young ladies can have patience to be so very accomplished as they all are.

MRS HURST. *All* young ladies accomplished! My dear Charles, what do you mean?

MR. BINGLEY. I am sure I never heard a young lady spoken of for the first time, without being informed that she was very accomplished.

MR. DARCY. I cannot boast of knowing more than half a dozen, in the whole range of my acquaintance, that are really accomplished.

CAROLINE BINGLEY. Nor I, I am sure.

ELIZABETH. Then you must comprehend a great deal in your idea of an accomplished woman.

CAROLINE BINGLEY. Oh! To be really accomplished, a woman must have a thorough knowledge of music, singing, drawing, dancing, and the modern languages and besides all this, she must possess a certain something in her air ...

(Mr. Darcy looks approvingly at Elizabeth Bennet's abandoned book. Caroline, moving to the piano, notices his appreciation of Miss Bennet and is jealous.)

MR. DARCY. And to all this she must yet add something more substantial: the improvement of her mind by extensive reading.

ELIZABETH. I am no longer surprised at your knowing only six accomplished women. I rather wonder now at your knowing any.

MR. DARCY. Are you so severe upon your own sex?

ELIZABETH. I've never seen such a woman. My apologies I must see to my sister.

(Elizabeth takes her leave, the men rise and she exits. Mr. Darcy stands for a moment longer than necessary as Elizabeth Bennet exits. His eyes follow her out.)

SCENE EIGHT

Mr. Darcy is snapped out of his reverie as Caroline Bingley begins singing and playing HOW SWEET IN THE WOODLANDS by Mr. Harrington in an obvious plan to try to divert his attention to herself.

CAROLINE BINGLEY.
>HOW SWEET IN THE WOODLANDS
>WITH FLEET, HOUND AND HORN
>TO WAKEN SHRILL ECHO
>AND TASTE THE FRESH MORN
>BUT HARD IS THE CHANCE
>MY FOND HEART MUST PURSUE

(Her eyes look to Mr. Darcy who has been looking after where Elizabeth left the room.)
>FOR DAPHNE, FAIR DAPHNE
>IS LOST TO MY VIEW

SHE'S LOST, FAIR DAPHNE
IS LOST TO MY VIEW

CAROLINE BINGLEY. Elizabeth Bennet is one of those young ladies who seek to recommend themselves to the other sex by undervaluing themselves and their sex. With many men, I dare say, it succeeds, but I'm sure you find such meanness contemptible, do you not, Mr. Darcy?

MR. DARCY. Undoubtedly, there is meanness in all the arts which ladies sometimes condescend to employ for the captivation of the opposite sex, do you not agree, Miss Bingley? *(Miss Bingley has been seen through and she blushes faintly. Elizabeth returns. The men stand.)*

ELIZABETH. I've come to bid you goodnight. My sister's fever has returned/

MR. BINGLEY. I'll call to town immediately for one of the most eminent physicians I know/

ELIZABETH. Oh, no please/

MR. BINGLEY. Or if you prefer, Mr. Jones will be sent for again early in the morning only if Miss Bennet is not decidedly better by then?

ELIZABETH. Thank you. Good night. *(Elizabeth exits. Mr. Darcy watches her go. Caroline resumes playing, despondently, capturing her unrequited feelings for Mr. Darcy as well as his growing feelings for Elizabeth.)*

CAROLINE BINGLEY.
SHE'S LOST, FAIR DAPHNE
IS - LOST TO MY VIEW

SCENE NINE

The next morning at Netherfield. Mrs. Bennet, Lydia and Kitty sit with the two Bingley sisters and Mr. Bingley. As a guest in the house, Mr. Darcy remains standing, apart from the others.

MR. BINGLEY. I hope, Mrs. Bennet, you've not found Miss Bennet worse than you expected.

MRS. BENNET. *(Melodramatically as usual.)* Indeed I have, sir. Mr. Jones says we must not think of moving her. We must trespass a little longer on your kindness.

MR. BINGLEY. My sister, I am sure, will not hear of her removal.

MRS. BENNET. She is very ill indeed, and suffers a vast deal, though with the greatest patience in the world, which is always the way with her, for she has the sweetest temper I ever met with. I often tell my other girls they are nothing to her. You have a sweet room here, Mr. Bingley. I do not know a place in the country that is equal to Netherfield. You will not think of quitting it in a hurry.

MR. BINGLEY. Whatever I do is done in a hurry but at present I consider myself as quite fixed here.

ELIZABETH. *(Gently.)* That is exactly what I should have supposed of you.

MRS. BENNET. Lizzy…

MR. BINGLEY. I did not know that you were a studier of character. It must be an amusing study.

MRS. BENNET. *(Masking her irritation.)* Oh, yes Elizabeth is a great studier of character.

ELIZABETH. *(Glancing unintentionally at Mr. Darcy.)* Yes; but intricate characters are the most amusing.

MR. DARCY. The country can in general supply but few subjects for such a study as you move in a very unvarying society.

ELIZABETH. But people themselves alter so much, that there is something new to be observed in them...forever.

MRS. BENNET. The country is a vast deal pleasanter than London, is not it, Mr. Bingley?

MR. BINGLEY. When I am in the country I never wish to leave it; and when I am in town it is pretty much the same. I can be equally happy in either.

MRS. BENNET. That is because you have the right disposition. But - that gentleman *(Referring to Mr. Darcy)* seems to think the country is nothing at all.

ELIZABETH. Indeed, Mama, you are mistaken. Mr. Darcy only meant that there was not such a variety of people to be met with in the country as in town, which you must acknowledge to be true.

MRS. BENNET. I'll have you know we dine with four-and-twenty families!

(The Bingley sisters stifle their amusement.) Often with our closest neighbor Sir William who always has something to say to everybody. That is my idea of good breeding; and those persons who fancy themselves very important and never open their mouths, quite mistake the matter. *(Rising to exit.)* I must thank you again for your kindness to Jane...and my apologies for troubling you with Elizabeth.

LYDIA. You promised, Mr. Bingley, to give a ball at Netherfield! It would be a most shameful thing if you did not keep your promise! *(Elizabeth is embarrassed.)*

BINGLEY. I am perfectly ready, I assure you, to keep my engagement; and when your sister is fully recovered, you shall, if you please, name the very day of the ball.

(They make their goodbyes. A servant comes with a note for Elizabeth and then speaks with Mr. Bingley who nods and exits with him/her. Caroline and Mrs. Hurst take Mr. Darcy's arms on either side and begin to walk. He turns back to Elizabeth.)

MR. DARCY. This walk is not wide enough for our party. We had better go into the avenue.

ELIZABETH. No, no! You are charmingly grouped. It would be spoilt by admitting a fourth. *(Waving the note.)* Jane will join us after dinner! *(Elizabeth runs off happily. Mr. Darcy watches her go as he is escorted off by the Bingley sisters.)*

SCENE TEN

Elizabeth enters with Jane who is wrapped up warmly. Mr. Bingley is attentive to Jane and they talk privately. Mrs. Hurst plays with her bracelets and rings and soon falls asleep as the others are intent on reading.

CAROLINE BINGLEY. How pleasant it is to spend an evening in this way! I declare there is no enjoyment like reading! *(Caroline yawns, throws aside her book, and* *walks about the room.)* Miss Eliza Bennet, let me persuade you to follow my example, and take a turn about the room. I assure you it is very refreshing after sitting so long. *(Lizzy joins Caroline Bingley. Mr. Darcy finally looks up and unconsciously closes his book and gazes at Elizabeth Bennet and she and Caroline walk around the room, arm in arm.)* Do, join us Mr. Darcy.

MR. DARCY. No, I think not. I can imagine but two motives for your choosing to walk up and down the room together; either of which my joining you would interfere.

CAROLINE BINGLEY. What could he mean?

MR. DARCY. You are either in each other's confidence, and have secret affairs to discuss, or you are conscious that your figures appear to the greatest advantage in walking.

CAROLINE BINGLEY. Oh! Shocking! How shall we punish him for such a speech?

ELIZABETH. Nothing so easy. Tease him. Laugh at him.

MR. DARCY. The wisest and the best of men's actions may be rendered ridiculous by a person whose first object in life - is a joke.

ELIZABETH. I hope I never ridicule what is wise and good. Follies and nonsense: I laugh at them whenever I can.

MR. DARCY. It has been the study of my life to avoid those weaknesses which often inspire ridicule.

ELIZABETH. Such as vanity and pride.

MR. DARCY. Yes, vanity is a weakness indeed. But pride — where there is a real superiority of mind, I should hope pride will be under good regulation.

CAROLINE BINGLEY. *(She is a bit lost trying to follow this discussion.)* Your examination of Mr. Darcy is over, I presume? Pray what is the result?

ELIZABETH. I am perfectly convinced that Mr. Darcy has no defect.

MR. DARCY. No, I have faults enough, but they are not, I hope, of understanding. But I cannot forget the follies and vices of others so soon as I ought, nor their offenses against myself. My good opinion once lost, is lost forever.

ELIZABETH. That is a failing indeed! But I cannot laugh at it.

MR. DARCY. There is, I believe, in every one a tendency to some particular evil — a natural defect, which not even the best education can overcome.

ELIZABETH. And your defect is to hate everybody.

MR. DARCY. And yours is to misunderstand them.

CAROLINE BINGLEY. Do let us have a little music! *(Mrs. Hurst is startled awake as Caroline Bingley plays the piano and sings HOW SWEET IN THE WOODLAND brightly, to liven the mood...)*

SCENE ELEVEN

(...and the Ensemble joins in singing as Jane and Elizabeth leave Netherfield. Mr. Bingley looks on after Jane. The girls arrive home to Longbourn.)

ENSEMBLE.
    HOW SWEET IN THE WOODLANDS
    WITH FLEET, HOUND AND HORN

TO WAKEN SHRILL ECHO
AND TASTE THE FRESH MORN
BUT HARD IS THE CHANCE
MY FOND HEART MUST PURSUE
FOR DAPHNE, FAIR DAPHNE
IS LOST TO MY VIEW
SHE'S LOST, FAIR DAPHNE
IS LOST TO MY VIEW

MR. BENNET. Oh Lizzy, Jane. I'm glad you are home. With your absence the conversation has lost much of its

animation, and most of its sense. My cousin, Mr. Collins has arrived.

ELIZABETH. Is he as absurd as you'd hoped?

KITTY. Oh mama, must we sit with Mr. Collins yet again...?

LYDIA. He insists on reading Fordyce's Sermons aloud...

(Mr. Collins talks with Mary and Mrs Bennet. Kitty and Lydia attempt to sit as far from Mr. Collins as possible. Introductions are made.)

MRS. BENNET. Jane, my eldest. And Elizabeth. Mr. Collins.

MR. COLLINS. You have a fine family of daughters. Fame of their beauty has fallen short of the truth and I've no doubt you will have them all in due time disposed of in marriage.

MRS. BENNET. I wish with all my heart it may prove so, for else they will be destitute enough. Things are settled so oddly.

MR. COLLINS. You allude, perhaps, to the entail of this estate. I am very sensible, madam, of the hardship to my fair cousins. Lady Catherine has advised me to marry as soon as I can, provided I choose with discretion... *(Eyeing the room.)* I could suppose myself in the small summer breakfast parlour at Rosings/

ELIZABETH *(To the audience.)* It would seem we are not the only objects of Mr. Collins's admiration...

MR. BENNET. *(Watches Elizabeth's reaction to what he's just unleashed.)* Mr. Collins is very fortunate, in his patroness, Lady Catherine de Bourgh.

MR. COLLINS. Oh, yes, indeed I am. I have never in my life witnessed such behaviour in a person of rank—such affability and condescension, as I have myself experienced from Lady Catherine. She has always spoken to me as she would to any other gentleman; she makes not the smallest objection to my joining in the society of the neighbourhood/

MRS. BENNET. I think you said she is a widow, sir? Has she any family?

MR. COLLINS. She has only one daughter, Miss Anne de Bourgh, the heiress of Rosings, and of very extensive property.

MRS. BENNET. Ah! Then she is better off than many girls. *(Hinting their home Longbourn which Mr. Collins will inherit.)* And what sort of young lady is she?

MR. COLLINS. She is a most charming young lady indeed. But as I told Lady Catherine one day, her indifferent state of health has deprived the British court of its brightest ornament. I am happy on every occasion to offer those little delicate compliments which are always acceptable to ladies.

(Mr. Bennet and Elizabeth are amused by his foppery.)

MR. BENNET. May I ask whether these pleasing attentions proceed from the impulse of the moment, or are the result of previous study?

MR. COLLINS. I sometimes amuse myself with suggesting and arranging such little elegant compliments as may be adapted to ordinary occasions, but I always wish to give them as unstudied an air as possible.

MRS. BENNET. Does Lady Catherine live near you, sir?

MR. COLLINS. The garden in which stands my humble abode is separated only by a lane from Rosings Park, her ladyship's residence.

LYDIA. Oh! *(Stifling a yawn)* Mama, you promised we could walk to Meryton to ask when Mr. Denny comes back from town.

MR. BENNET. Oh, what a fine idea. Mr. Collins you must accompany my daughters to town. I'll be in my library, my dear…*(He escapes.)*

SCENE TWELVE

Lizzy, Jane, Lydia and Kitty walk into Meryton singing happily, lively. Mr. Collins struggles to keep up.

THE BENNET SISTERS.
    HOW SWEET IN THE WOODLANDS
    WITH FLEET, HOUND AND HORN

TO WAKEN SHRILL ECHO
AND TASTE THE FRESH MORN/

KITTY. Lydia, it's Mr. Denny!

LYDIA. And Mr. Wickham! *(Lydia and Kitty move further off to giggle with the officers and meet Mr. Wickham who stands out from the rest. Mrs. Phillips enters with a basket as she has been shopping in town and is introduced to Mr. Collins. Opposite, Mr. Bingley and Mr. Darcy enter, bow courteously and stop to speak with Jane and Elizabeth.)*

MR. BINGLEY. Good day, Miss Bennet. Miss Elizabeth. We were on our way to Longbourn to invite you personally to the Netherfield ball.

(Mr. Bingley hands Jane an invitation. Mr. Darcy corroborates this with a bow, and then sees Mr. Wickham. Mr. Wickham touches his hat — a salutation which Mr. Darcy just deigns to return with a small nod of his head. Mr. Darcy then bows to the ladies and quickly exits.)

ELIZABETII. What could be the meaning of it?

JANE. It is impossible to imagine…. *(Mr. Bingley, clearly troubled for his friend, takes his leave politely and follows after him.)*

LYDIA. Oh, Mr. Wickham! *(Lydia laughs loudly and whispers something in his ear. Wickham laughs, then shakes his finger at her, still laughing, and exits the opposite way Mr. Darcy has. Lydia and Kitty return to Jane and Elizabeth. Seeing the invitation.)* Look! The invitation to the Netherfield ball. I chose the date you know! Next week! And *tomorrow* evening some of the officers are to dine with the Phillipses and we are invited.

KITTY. *(Giggling.)* Even Mr. Collins is invited! And Lydia made quite sure the *new* officer is coming of course/

SCENE THIRTEEN

The scene turns swiftly to the following evening at the Phillipses as Mr. Wickham enters with other officers.

KITTY. …Mr. Wickham! *(Mr. Collins is busy telling Mr. and Mrs. Phillips loudly and proudly all about Rosings. Mr. Phillips stands pretentiously "breathing port wine.")*

MR. COLLINS. Rosings borders the park nearly opposite the front of the Parsonage... *(All the women gawk at Mr. Wickham. He ends up seated beside Elizabeth and Lydia, who is very much occupied with lottery tickets.)*

LYDIA. Oh, I am so fond of a nice comfortable noisy game of lottery tickets!

MR. COLLINS. Lady Catherine once upon a visit to my humble parsonage vouchsafed to suggest — herself — some shelves in the upstairs closet...

ELIZABETH. *(To the audience.)* Shelves in a closet, a happy thought indeed.

MR. WICKHAM. Have you known Mr. Darcy long?

ELIZABETH. About a month. He is a man of very large property in Derbyshire, I understand.

MR. WICKHAM. Yes, his estate, Pemberley, is a noble one. You could not have met with a person more capable of giving you certain information on that head than myself, for I have been connected with Mr. Darcy and his family from my infancy. The greatest part of our youth was passed together. My father devoted all his time to the care of the Pemberley property and was most highly esteemed by the late Mr. Darcy *(pause)* You may well be surprised, Miss Bennet, at such an assertion, after seeing the very cold manner of our meeting yesterday. Are you much acquainted with Mr. Darcy?

ELIZABETH. As much as I ever wish to be. He is not at all liked in Hertfordshire.

MR. WICKHAM. I cannot pretend to be sorry. I wonder whether he is likely to be in this county much longer.

ELIZABETH. I do not at all know, but I hope your plans will not be affected by his being in the neighbourhood.

MR. WICKHAM. Oh! no — it is not for me to be driven away by Mr. Darcy. If he wishes to avoid seeing me, he must go. His father, Miss Bennet, the late Mr Darcy, was one of the best men that ever breathed. I could forgive his son anything rather than disgrace the memory of his father. I have been a disappointed man. A military life is not what I was intended for. The church ought to have been my profession.

ELIZABETH. Indeed!

MR. WICKHAM. Yes — the late Mr. Darcy bequeathed me the living... but when the living fell, it was given elsewhere.

ELIZABETH. Good heavens! But how could that be?

MR. WICKHAM. Had the late Mr. Darcy liked me less, his son might have borne with me better; but his father's uncommon attachment to me irritated him, I believe, and he hates me.

ELIZABETH. Though I have never liked him. I had not thought so very ill of him. *(pause)* What sort of girl is his sister, Miss Darcy?

MR. WICKHAM. She is too much like her brother — very, very proud. She is a handsome girl, about sixteen and I understand, highly accomplished.

LYDIA. I've won!

MR. COLLINS. Why yes, the chimney-piece at Rosings alone cost eight hundred pounds!

MR. WICKHAM. You know of course that Mr. Collins's patroness, Lady Catherine de Bourgh and Lady Anne Darcy were sisters; consequently that she is aunt to the present Mr. Darcy.

ELIZABETH. No, indeed, I did not. Mr. Collins speaks highly of Lady Catherine; but I suspect his gratitude misleads him, and she is an arrogant, conceited woman.

MR. WICKHAM. I believe Lady Catherine to be both in a great degree. Her daughter, Miss Anne de Bourgh, will have a very large fortune, and it is believed that she and her cousin will unite the two estates. *(pause)* Why do you smile?

ELIZABETH. *(To the audience)* Poor Miss "highly accomplished" Caroline Bingley. Her attentions on Mr Darcy - her reading, her piano playing - are all in vain.

SCENE FOURTEEN

The family and Mr. Collins return to Longbourn. Elizabeth tells Jane everything she has learned about Mr. Darcy and Mr. Wickham.

JANE. Can Mr. Darcy's most intimate friends be so deceived in him? *(pause)* Lizzy?! Lizzy...
ELIZABETH. *(To the audience.)* I can think of nothing but of Mr. Wickham.
JANE. Mr. Bingley cannot know what Mr. Darcy is...Lizzy?!
ELIZABETH. I cannot believe Mr. Wickham should invent such a history of himself. *(To the audience)* There was truth in his looks.
LYDIA. Look Mary, I won seven fish! And Kitty only three! But I do prefer dancing! Oh, Lord! How I should like to be married before any of you and I could chaperone you and Kitty to the Netherfield ball next week. Even Mary wishes to go now!
MARY BENNET. While I can have my mornings to myself I think it is no sacrifice to join occasionally in evening engagements/
KITTY. Especially when it's a ball at/

SCENE FIFTEEN

They enter Netherfield.

KITTY. …Netherfield!

MR. COLLINS. I shall hope to be honoured with the hands of all my fair cousins in the course of the evening; and I take this opportunity of soliciting yours, Miss Elizabeth, for the first dance especially.

(Elizabeth is stunned at the thought of dancing with him. Lydia and Kitty avoid him. Elizabeth searches the room for Mr. Wickham. Lydia joins her.)

LYDIA. Oh, Lizzy. You won't find Mr. Wickham, I'm afraid. Mr. Denny told us that he had been obliged to go to town on business.

ELIZABETH. *(To the audience.)* Or perhaps he wished to avoid a certain gentleman here...as I do...

(She tries to avoid Mr. Collins and Mr. Darcy, but Mr. Darcy moves toward her.)

MR. DARCY. Would you do me the honor of the next dance, Miss Bennet?

(She nods her consent. He bows and moves away. She is vexed.)

ELIZABETH. But I am determined to hate him!

CHARLOTTE LUCAS. Do not to be a simpleton, Eliza! He's a man ten times the consequence of Mr. Wickham!

(They greet Mr. Bingley and his sisters. Mr. Collins moves to her. She takes his hand. It is very awkward. They all

form lines for the first dance. Mr. Collins bumps into Elizabeth and then moves in the wrong direction, finding himself outside of the formation; Mr. Darcy steps into his place. Mr. Collins moves sycophantically away. Elizabeth is surprised but half-relieved as well. They dance. After a few moments of silence.)

ELIZABETH. So you enjoy a dance once you're acquainted with your partner, Mr. Darcy?

MR. DARCY. *(warmly)* I do indeed.

ELIZABETH. *(pause)* Perhaps by and by I may observe that private balls are much pleasanter than public ones.

MR. DARCY. Do you talk by rule, then, while you are dancing?

ELIZABETH. It would look odd to be entirely silent.

MR. DARCY. Do you walk often to Meryton?

ELIZABETH. Oh yes. When you met us the other day, we had just been forming a new acquaintance: Mr. Wickham.

MR. DARCY. Yes. Mr. Wickham is blessed with such happy manners as may ensure his making friends — whether he may be equally capable of retaining them, is less certain.

ELIZABETH. He has been so unlucky as to lose your friendship and in a manner which he is likely to suffer from all his life. I remember hearing you say, Mr. Darcy, that your resentment once created was unappeasable. You are very cautious, I suppose, as to its being created?

MR. DARCY. I am.

ELIZABETH. And never allow yourself to be blinded by prejudice?

MR. DARCY. I hope not. May I ask to what these questions tend?

ELIZABETH. Merely to the illustration of your character. I am trying to make it out.

MR. DARCY. And what is your success?

ELIZABETH. I do not get on at all. I hear such different accounts of you as puzzle me exceedingly.

MR. DARCY. I can readily believe that reports may vary greatly with respect to me; and I could wish, Miss Bennet, that you were not to sketch my character at the present moment, as there is reason to fear that the performance would reflect no credit on either of us.

ELIZABETH. But if I do not take your likeness now, I may never have another opportunity.

MR. DARCY. I would by no means suspend any pleasure of yours.

ELIZABETH. *(An awkward pause.)* And now, we may be silent. *(They go down the dance, moving coolly away from each other. Mrs. Bennet is gossiping. Mr. Bennet is trying to keep her in check. Mary begins to play a lively version of ROBIN ADAIR. She sings poorly. Snippets of the song are overheard between the various bits of dialogue.)*

MARY.
> WHAT'S THIS DULL TOWN TO ME?
> ROBIN'S NOT NEAR

MRS. BENNET. I cautioned Mr. Collins against it!

MARY.
> WHAT WAS'T I WISH'D TO SEE?
> WHAT WISH'D TO HEAR?

MRS. BENNET. Jane is soon to be engaged!

MARY.

> WHERE'S ALL THE JOY AND MIRTH
> MADE THIS TOWN A HEAV'N ON EARTH?

MRS. BENNET. And it was soon done!

MARY.

> OH, THEY'RE ALL FLED WITH THEE
> ROBIN ADAIR

MR. BENNET. What was soon done, madam?

MARY.

> WHAT MADE THE ASSEMBLY SHINE?
> ROBIN WAS THERE

MRS. BENNET. Mr. Collins had only to change from Jane to Elizabeth!

MARY.

> WHAT MADE THE BALL SO FINE?
> ROBIN WAS THERE

MRS. BENNET. Bingley is such a charming man!

(Mary plays on. Mr. Collins corners Elizabeth.)

MR. COLLINS. I have found out that there is now in the room a near relation of my patroness. Mr. Darcy. I shall pay my respects to him.

ELIZABETH. You are not going to introduce yourself? To Mr. Darcy!

MR. COLLINS. Indeed I am. My dear Miss Elizabeth, I have the highest opinion in the world of your excellent judgment in all matters within the scope of your understanding/

ELIZABETH. I assure your Mr. Darcy would consider your addressing him without introduction as impertinence rather than a compliment to his aunt.

MRS. BENNET. So rich, and living but three miles from Longbourn! *(And with a low bow Mr. Collins leaves Elizabeth to introduce himself with a deep bow to Mr. Darcy who eyes him with unrestrained wonder. Mary's music plays on and overlaps with Mr. Collins and Mrs. Bennet's monologues of which we hear only part.)*
MR. COLLINS. It is with the greatest honour to inform you that/
MRS. BENNET. Jane will soon be married/
MARY. LA, LA, LA, LA, LA, LA…

MRS. BENNET. …to Mr. Bingley!
MR. COLLINS. Your Aunt, my patroness/
MARY. LA, LA, LA, LA, LA, LA…
MRS. BENNET. That will throw the girls in the path of other rich young men!
MR. COLLINS. Lady Catherine de Bourgh was quite well when I last left Kent/
(Mr. Darcy does not respond. Mr. Collins makes another steep bow. The awkwardness of the introduction is palpable. Mr. Darcy nods and turns back to his friends who do their best to stifle their shock and amusement at Mr. Collins having introduced himself in this way.)
MRS. BENNET. *(Loudly.)* But that proud gentleman...
ELIZABETH. Mother, please...!
MRS. BENNET. What is Mr. Darcy to me, pray, that I should be afraid of him?
MR. BENNET. For heaven's sake, madam, speak lower. *(Mary starts the refrain once again. Jane and Elizabeth exchange worried glances.)*

MR. BENNET. *(To Mary)* That will do extremely well, child. You have delighted us long enough. Let the other young ladies have time to exhibit.
(Lydia, Kitty and Mrs. Forster laugh loudly at some joke. The officers are amused. The Bingley sisters are not. Jane and Bingley's eyes meet; he turns suddenly and exits with Mr. Darcy and the Bingley sisters.)
ELIZABETH. *(To the audience.)* Had my family made an agreement to expose themselves as much as they could during the evening, it would have been impossible for them to play their parts with more spirit or finer success.

SCENE SIXTEEN

The scene returns to the next morning at Longbourn. Mary practices the piano: HOW MISTAKEN IS THE LOVER)

MARY.
> HOW MISTAKEN IS THE LOVER
> WHO ON WORDS BUILDS HOPES OF BLISS
> AND FONDLY THINKS WE LOVE DISCOVER

LYDIA. *(yawning loudly)* Lord, how tired I am!
MARY.
> AND FONDLY THINKS WE LOVE DISCOVER

LYDIA.   Oh, Mary do you have to practice so early!?
MARY.
> IF PERCHANCE WE ANSWER …

(Mr. Collins approaches Mrs. Bennet.)
MR COLLINS. May I, madam, solicit a private audience with your fair daughter Elizabeth?

MARY.

    OFF THE TONGUE, THE HEART BELYING
    DARES NOT VENTURE ON DENYING

MRS. BENNET. Oh yes! Certainly. Kitty, up stairs!

ELIZABETH. Oh, do not go. I beg you will not go. I am going away myself!

MARY.

    OFF THE TONGUE, THE HEART BELYING,
    DARES NOT VENTURE ON DENYING

MRS. BENNET. Lizzy. Stay where you are.

MARY.

    BUT, IN SPITE OF
    DISCONTENT,
    GIVES THE
    SEMBLANCE
    OF CONTENT.

MRS. BENNET. I insist upon your staying and hearing Mr. Collins! Mary!

(Everyone exits the room leaving Mr. Collins with Elizabeth, who sits in silence.)

MR. COLLINS. My dear Miss Elizabeth. Almost as soon as I entered the house, I singled you out as the companion of my future life. But before I am run away with by my feelings on this subject, perhaps it would be advisable for me to state my reasons for marrying…

(Elizabeth tries not to laugh openly. Mrs. Bennet, the sisters and servants listen in. Mr. Collins is oblivious.)

MR. COLLINS. My reasons for marrying are, first, that I think it a right thing for every clergyman to set the example of matrimony in his parish; secondly, that I am convinced that it will add greatly to my happiness; and thirdly it is the particular recommendation of the Lady Catherine de Bourgh. And now nothing remains for me but to assure you in the most animated language of the violence of my affection.

ELIZABETH. You are too hasty, sir. You forget that I have made no answer. Accept my thanks for the compliment you are paying me but it is impossible for me to do otherwise than to decline them.

MR. COLLINS. *(Charmed, thinking she is playing a game with him.)* I know it to be the custom of your sex to reject a man on the first application.

ENSEMBLE.
> AH! HOW VAIN IS ART'S PROFESSION
> THOUGH THE FALTERING TONGUE COMPLY!
> WHAT AVAILS THE COLD CONFESSION,
> IF THE AVERTED EYES DENY!

(Tension increases as Mr. Collins is determined)
> HAPPIER FAR, THE EXPERIENCED SWAIN
> KNOWS HE TRIUMPH MUST ATTAIN,
> WHEN IN VAIN SUCCESS-LESS TRIAL,
> LANGUAGE GIVES THE FAINT DENIAL
> THE FAINT DENIAL, THE FAINT DENIAL

ELIZABETH. I am perfectly serious in my refusal. You could not make me happy. And I am the last woman in the world who could make you so.

MR. COLLINS. In spite of your manifold attractions, it is by no means certain that another offer of marriage may ever be made you.

ELIZABETH. I thank you again for your proposal but my feelings in every respect forbid it.

ENSEMBLE.

> WHILE THE EYES BETRAY THE FICTION
> IN DELIGHTFUL CONTRADICTION;
> AND THE CHEEKS WITH BLUSHES GLOW.
> AND THE TONGUE STILL FALTERS "NO".

ELIZABETH. Can I speak plainer? Do not consider me now as an elegant female, intending to plague you, but as a rational creature, speaking the truth from her heart.

MR. COLLINS. You are uniformly charming! I am by no means discouraged and shall hope to lead you to the altar ere long.

(Mrs. Bennet rushes in. Elizabeth exits to find her father.)

MRS. BENNET. Lizzy has refused you? Headstrong, foolish girl...

(Mr. Collins exits. Mr. Bennet and Lizzy enter.)

MRS. BENNET. Oh! Mr Bennet! You must come and make Lizzy marry Mr. Collins

MR. BENNET. And what am I to do on the occasion? It seems an hopeless business.

MRS. BENNET. Tell her that you insist upon her marrying him or I will never see her again.

MR. BENNET. An unhappy alternative is before you, Elizabeth. From this day you must be a stranger to one of your parents. Your mother will never see you again if you do not marry Mr. Collins, and I will never see you again if you do.

MRS. BENNET. Oh, Mr. Bennet!

(The sisters/servants, who have been listening in, enter.)

ENSEMBLE.

> HOW MISTAKEN IS THE LOVER
> WHO ON WORDS BUILDS HOPES OF BLISS
> AND FONDLY THINKS WE LOVE DISCOVER
> IF PERCHANCE SHE ANSWERS "YES"
> IF PERCHANCE SHE ANSWERS "YES"
> IF PERCHANCE SHE ANSWERS

(Ensemble waits for her reply...)

ELIZABETH. No!

SCENE SEVENTEEN

MRS. BENNET. Oh! Mr. Collins! I tell you, Miss Lizzy — if you go on refusing every offer of marriage in this way, you will never get a husband at all — and I am sure I do not know who is to maintain you when your father is dead. Oh, nobody feels for my poor nerves! Oh, and Charlotte Lucas is here! *(Enter Charlotte Lucas.)* And now I shall never hear the end of it from Lady Lucas...!

LYDIA. I am glad you are come, Charlotte, for there is such fun here this morning! Mr. Collins has made an offer to Lizzy, and she will not have him. And now we must go for a walk/

MRS. BENNET. In the shrubbery!

(Charlotte walks with and listens to Mr. Collins as the others avoid his company.)

MR. COLLINS. I have certainly meant well… *(The Bennet sisters walk in the shrubbery. Charlotte and Mr. Collins exit together. Mr. Wickham and Mr. Denny enter.)*

LYDIA. Lizzy! It's Mr. Wickham, coming down the lane to Longbourn!

KITTY. And Mr. Denny! *(Mr. Wickham moves beside Elizabeth. Lydia listens in. Kitty chats happily with Mr. Denny.)*

MR. WICKHAM. I can only my offer my apologies for missing the opportunity of dancing with you at the Netherfield ball. I found that to be in the same room with the gentleman might be more than I could bear, and that scenes might arise unpleasant to more than myself... *(Mr. Wickham bows and leaves. Charlotte enters the shrubbery to speak with Elizabeth while Mr. Collins looks smugly on. A servant hands Mrs. Bennet a letter. The two scenes happen simultaneously.)*

MRS. BENNET. *(Reading)* A letter, from Lady Lucas...? Charlotte Lucas is...

ELIZABETH. Engaged to Mr. Collins! My dear Charlotte - impossible!

CHARLOTTE LUCAS. Because he was not so happy as to succeed with you? I am not romantic, you know; I never was. I am convinced that my chance of happiness with

him is as fair as most people can boast on entering the
marriage state.
ELIZABETH. I wish you all imaginable happiness....

SCENE EIGHTEEN

*(The Ensemble gathers, animated with the prospect of an
engagement. Beaming with self-importance, Mr. Collins
hands Charlotte a small bunch of flowers. Charlotte turns
to him as if in a wedding ceremony. All await her reply.)*

ENSEMBLE.
> OFF THE TONGUE, THE HEART BELYING,
> DARES NOT VENTURE ON DENYING
> BUT, IN SPITE OF DISCONTENT,
> GIVES THE SEMBLANCE OF CONTENT.
>
> HOW MISTAKEN IS THE LOVER
> WHO ON WORDS BUILDS HOPES OF BLISS
> AND FONDLY THINKS WE LOVE DISCOVER
> IF PERCHANCE SHE ANSWERS "YES"
> IF PERCHANCE SHE ANSWERS "YES"
> IF PERCHANCE SHE ANSWERS

CHARLOTTE. *(Pause. Resignedly.)* Yes.
(Charlotte and Mr. Collins wave goodbye.)
ENSEMBLE. (Slower.)
> BUT, IN SPITE OF DISCONTENT,
> GIVES THE SEMBLANCE OF CONTENT.

CHARLOTTE. *(To Elizabeth.)* Promise me to come to Hunsford! *(Mr. and Mrs. Collins exit.)*

SCENE NINETEEN

Jane walks alone as the seasons pass. It is winter. Approaching Christmas. GREENSLEEVES is sung quietly by the Ensemble as they deck the halls of Longbourn.

ENSEMBLE.
> ALAS MY LOVE YOU DO ME WRONG
> TO CAST ME OFF SO DISCOURTEOUSLY;
> AND I HAVE LOVED YOU SO LONG
> DELIGHTING IN YOUR COMPANY.
>
> GREENSLEEVES WAS ALL MY JOY
> GREENSLEEVES MY DELIGHT
> GREENSLEEVES WAS MY HEART OF GOLD
> AND WHO BUT MY LADY GREENSLEEVES

(Ensemble hums softly like carolers beneath the dialogue.)

MRS. BENNET. Oh, Mr. Bennet it is very hard to think that I should live to see Charlotte Lucas take her place in this house! *(A servant delivers a note.)*

MR. BENNET. It is Christmas. Be of good cheer, my dear. Let us hope for better things. Let us flatter ourselves that *I* may be the survivor.

MRS. BENNET. And Mr. Bingley leaving Netherfield so suddenly!? Oh but he must be down again in the summer... *(Reading her letter.)* Oh, Mr. Bennet, my brother Mr.

Gardiner and his wife will spend Christmas with us here at Longbourn! *(Jane and Elizabeth talk privately.)*

JANE. She can have no idea of the pain she gives me by her continual reflections on Mr. Bingley. But it cannot last long. He will be forgot, and we shall all be as we were before. *(Sighs.)* I have this comfort that it has not been more than an error of fancy on my side, and that it has done no harm to anyone but myself.

ELIZABETH. My dear Jane, you are too good. *(To the audience)* There are few people whom I really love, and still fewer of whom I think well. *(To Jane)* The more I see of the world, the more am I dissatisfied with it; and every day confirms my belief of the inconsistency of all human characters, and of the little dependence that can be placed on the appearance of merit - Mr. Bingley?- or sense! Jane! Mr. Collins is a conceited, pompous, narrow-minded, silly man: you know he is, as well as I do; and you must feel, as well as I do, that the woman who marries him cannot have a proper way of thinking!

JANE. Enough of this! Believe, for everybody's sake, that she may feel something like regard and esteem for our cousin. *(Pause.)* You persist, then, in supposing Mr. Bingley's sisters influenced him?

ELIZABETH. Yes, in conjunction with his friend, Mr. Darcy.

JANE. Lizzy, please... I am not ashamed of having been mistaken in Mr. Bingley's regard for me. *(She stops Lizzy from interrupting her.)* It is nothing in comparison of what I should feel in thinking ill of him or his sisters. Let me take it in the best light, in the light in which it may be understood. *(Elizabeth agrees. Much merriment and music as Christmas arrives and Mrs. Bennet welcomes the officers and the Gardiners. Presents are distributed, the Bennet girls and officers dance. The music begins, perhaps hammered out by Mary at the piano, while Wickham charms all by playing the flute/tin whistle along to DRIVE THE COLD WINTER AWAY.)*

ENSEMBLE.

 ALL HAIL TO THE DAYS
 THAT MERIT MORE PRAISE
 THAN ALL THE REST OF THE YEAR,
 AND WELCOME THE NIGHTS
 THAT DOUBLE DELIGHTS,
 AS WELL FOR THE POOR AS THE PEER!

 GOOD FORTUNE ATTEND
 EACH MERRY MAN'S FRIEND,
 THAT DOTH BUT THE BEST THAT HE MAY;
 FORGETTING ALL WRONGS,
 WITH POEMS AND SONGS,
 TO DRIVE THE COLD WINTER AWAY.

MRS. GARDINER. *(To Lizzy.)* Poor Jane! She may not get over this heartbreak immediately. You, Lizzy, would have laughed yourself out of it. A change of scene might be of service. Do you think Jane would come to London?

ELIZABETH. Oh, Aunt. I think it the very thing Jane needs! *(Lizzy sees Wickham. Mrs. Gardiner notices.)*

MRS. GARDINER. I have nothing to say against Mr. Wickham; if he had the fortune he ought to have, I should

think you could not do better. But as it is, you must not let
your fancy run away with you.

ELIZABETH. At present, I am not in love with Mr.
Wickham; But he is, the most agreeable man I ever saw.
All I can promise you, is I will do my best.

ENSEMBLE.

> OLD GRUDGES FORGOT,
> ARE PUT IN THE POT,
> ALL SORROWS ASIDE THEY LAY,
> THE OLD AND THE YOUNG
> WITH CAROL AND SONG,
> TO DRIVE THE COLD WINTER AWAY.

*(Jane leaves with Mr. and Mrs. Gardiner. The music fades
into the next scene. Mrs Bennet and a servant or two come
and go, clearing the Christmas decorations.)*

SCENE TWENTY

*Elizabeth reads the letters from Jane who joins her
opposite on the stage to recite them as she is writing them
from London. Mrs. Bennet, calls to Elizabeth from off
stage. (Letters may be delivered by servants as they tidy
away the Christmas decorations from the scene prior.)*

MRS. BENNET. *(Off stage)* Lizzy? What news of Jane?

ELIZABETH. Jane writes of their safe arrival in London!

JANE. "I have been a week in town without either seeing
or hearing from Caroline."

MRS. BENNET. *(Popping her head in.)* Lizzy? What news?

ELIZABETH. Jane will be calling on Caroline Bingley in Grosvenor Street!

(Elizabeth reads as Jane recites the contents of her own letter to Elizabeth.)

JANE. "Caroline Bingley was very glad to see me, and reproached me for giving her no notice of my coming to London. My last letter must never have reached her."

ELIZABETH. *(To herself)* Oh, Jane! You wish to think all the world respectable.

MRS. BENNET. Lizzy? What news?

JANE. "Their brother is much engaged with Mr. Darcy that they scarcely ever see him. Miss Darcy was expected to dinner so my visit was not long."

ELIZABETH. *(To her mother)* Jane writes that she expects them to visit her soon.

(A servant hands Elizabeth yet another letter.)

JANE. "After waiting at home every morning for a fortnight, Caroline did at last visit. But it was very evident that she had no pleasure in it; she made no apology for not calling before and said not a word of wishing to see me again."

MRS. BENNET. Lizzy? What news?

JANE. "Mr. Bingley knows nothing of my being in town, I am certain, from something she said herself."

MRS. BENNET. Lizzy? What does Jane write?

ELIZABETH. *(to her mother)* She...thinks only of what will make her happy: our affection and the invariable kindness of our dear uncle and aunt.

JANE. "Let me hear from you very soon. Miss Bingley said something of them never returning to Netherfield again. Pray go to see your friend Charlotte at Hunsford. Yours, Jane" -- Our dear Aunt asks for news of Mr. Wickham/ *(Speaking simultaneously.)*
JANE. *(Worried.)* Oh Lizzy...
MRS. BENNET. *(Excited.)* Oh Lizzy!
(Mrs. Bennet enters with another letter in hand. The following news of the invitation to the lakes is shared with Jane as Mrs. Gardiner joins her to read Eliza's letter.)
ALL THREE. Mr. and Mrs. Gardiner invite you to accompany them on a tour of the lakes this summer!
ELIZABETH / JANE. Oh, what happiness!
ELIZABETH. *(To the audience.)* What are young men to rocks and mountains? *(Elizabeth and Mrs. Bennet exit.)*

SCENE TWENTY-ONE

Mrs. Gardiner and Jane continue reading Lizzy's letter. Mr. Wickham enters with Mary King who blushes at his attentions to her.

MRS. GARDINER. What news from Lizzy, Jane?
JANE. *(reading)* "Dear Aunt and dearest Jane, Mr. Wickham's attentions are over. The sudden acquisition of ten thousand pounds was the most remarkable charm of a Miss Mary King to whom he is now rendering himself agreeable; I am now convinced, my dear aunt, that I have never been much in love; for then I should at present

detest his very name. Kitty and Lydia take his defection much more to heart than I do. They are not yet open to the mortifying conviction that handsome young men must have something to live on as well as the plain. *(Pause.)* Summer and the lakes seem very far away...but January and February will pass and March will take me to Hunsford, to see: *(Jane and Mrs. Gardiner exit as...)*

SCENE TWENTY-TWO

Elizabeth arrives at the Parsonage where Mr. Collins has been gardening. Charlotte wears an apron. They exchange greetings.

ELIZABETH. Charlotte!

CHARLOTTE LUCAS. Welcome, my dear Eliza!

MR. COLLINS. Welcome to our humble abode. The cottage as you see is comfortable and the garden is large and well laid out. Note the neatness of the entrance and *(Pause.)* its view of Rosings!

CHARLOTTE LUCAS. Very few days pass in which Mr. Collins does not walk to Rosings or is not working in his garden, *(slyly)* an occupation which I encourage as much as possible.

MR. COLLINS. We dine at Rosings twice every week, and are never allowed to walk home. One of her ladyship's carriages is regularly ordered for us/ *(Sound of a horse clip-clopping along. He exits in anticipation.)*

CHARLOTTE LUCAS. Lady Catherine is a most attentive neighbour/
MR. COLLINS. *(Popping back in.)* Oh, pray make haste! There is such a sight to be seen!
(He then exits again hurriedly. Charlotte and Elizabeth move to stand and admire the view of the phaeton from the front window— between us and
them, invisible.)

CHARLOTTE LUCAS.
(Unsurprised.) Ah, Miss de Bourgh in her phaeton. *(Charlotte slowly removes her apron.)* I am indebted daily to Mr. Collins for the knowledge of what carriages go past on our lane, and how often especially Miss de Bourgh drives by in her phaeton, which he never fails to come and inform me of, though it happens almost every day.
(She exits to join Mr. Collins off stage.)
ELIZABETH. *(To the audience.)* I like Miss de Bourgh's appearance. She looks sickly and cross. Yes, she will make Mr. Darcy a very proper wife. *(Pause.)* When Mr. Collins can be forgotten, there is really an air of great comfort throughout the cottage, and by Charlotte's evident enjoyment of it -- her housekeeping, her parish and her poultry -- I suppose he must often be forgotten.
(Charlotte and Mr. Collins return.)
CHARLOTTE LUCAS. Well, my dear Eliza, the whole party has been asked to dine at Rosings tomorrow.

MR. COLLINS. Do not make yourself uneasy, my dear cousin, Lady Catherine will not think the worse of you for being simply dressed. Lady Catherine knows/

SCENE TWENTY-THREE

The scene turns quickly to Rosings. For tea.

LADY CATHERINE. …your father's estate is entailed on Mr. Collins, I think. For your sake, Charlotte, I am glad of it; but otherwise I see no occasion for entailing estates from the female line. It was not thought necessary in Sir Lewis de Bourgh's family. Do you play and sing, Miss Bennet?

ELIZABETH. A little.

LADY CATHERINE. Oh! Then, some time or other we shall be happy to hear you. Our instrument is a capital one, probably superior to — Do your sisters also play and sing?

ELIZABETH. One of them does.

LADY CATHERINE. You ought all to have learned. Has your governess left you?

ELIZABETH. We never had a governess.

LADY CATHERINE. No governess! Five daughters brought up at home without a governess! Are any of your younger sisters out, Miss Bennet?

ELIZABETH. Yes, ma'am, all.

LADY CATHERINE. All! What, all five out at once? The younger ones out before the elder ones are married!?

ELIZABETH. I think it would be very hard upon younger sisters, ma'am, that they should not have their share of society and amusement, because the elder may not have the means or inclination to marry early.

LADY CATHERINE. Upon my word, you give your opinion very decidedly for so young a person. Pray, what is your age? You cannot be more than twenty, I am sure.

ELIZABETH. I am not one-and-twenty.

LADY CATHERINE. Indeed. The weather promises to be fine tomorrow. My nephew, Mr. Darcy, is expected here in the course of a few weeks along with his cousin/

SCENE TWENTY-FOUR

Following swiftly on from the previous scene, two weeks later. Colonel Fitzwilliam and Mr. Darcy enter, bowing.

MR. DARCY. …Colonel Fitzwilliam. Miss Elizabeth Bennet. *(A long, awkward silence follows.)* Are you pleased with Kent, Miss Bennet?

ELIZABETH. Yes, Thank you.

MR. DARCY. And your family, they are well?

ELIZABETH. Yes, thank you. *(Pause.)* My eldest sister has been in town these three months. Have you never happened to see her there?

MR. DARCY. No, I have not been so fortunate.

(He nods and moves to his speak with his Aunt and Anne.)

COLONEL FITZWILLIAM. Mr. Darcy has told me much of you, Miss Bennet. I believe you are fond of music. Do you know this piece?
(Elizabeth is surprised to have been spoken of and to meet a cousin so easygoing. He encourages her to play THEIR GROVES OF SWEET MYRTLE by Robert Burns.)
LADY CATHERINE. What is that you are saying, Fitzwilliam? Are you talking? What are you telling Miss Bennet?
COLONEL FITZWILLIAM. We are speaking of music, madam.
(Elizabeth begins to play.)
LADY CATHERINE. Then I must have my share in the conversation if you are speaking of music. There are few people in England, I suppose, who have more true enjoyment of music than myself, or a better natural taste. If I had ever learnt, I should have been a great proficient. And so would Anne, if her health had allowed it. How does Georgiana get on, Darcy? She cannot expect to excel if she does not practice a good deal.
MR. DARCY. I assure you, madam she practises very constantly.
LADY CATHERINE. I have told Miss Bennet several times these past weeks, that she will never play really well unless she practises more; I have told her to come to Rosings every day, and play on the pianoforte in Mrs. Jenkinson's room. She would be in nobody's way, you know, in that part of the house.
(Mr. Darcy is ashamed of his Aunt's behavior. Elizabeth plays on. Mr. Darcy approaches, watches as she plays.)

ELIZABETH. You mean to frighten me, Mr. Darcy, by coming in all this state to hear me? But I will not be alarmed, though your sister does play so well. There is a stubbornness about me that never can bear to be frightened at the will of others. My courage always rises with every attempt to intimidate me.

MR. DARCY. I shall not say that you are mistaken because you could not really believe me to entertain any design of alarming you; and I have had the pleasure of your acquaintance long enough to know, that you find great enjoyment in occasionally professing opinions which, in fact, are not your own.

ELIZABETH. Your cousin will teach you not to believe a word I say. It is provoking me to retaliate, and such things may come out as will shock your relations to hear.

COLONEL FITZWILLIAM. Pray let me hear. I should like to know how he behaves among strangers.

ELIZABETH. Prepare yourself for something very dreadful. The first time of my ever seeing him at a ball in Hertfordshire, he refused to dance though gentlemen were scarce; and more than one young lady was sitting down in want of a partner.

MR. DARCY. I had not at that time the honour of knowing any lady in the assembly beyond my own party.

ELIZABETH. And nobody can ever be introduced at a ball.

MR. DARCY. I have not the talent which some people possess of conversing easily with those I have never seen before.

ELIZABETH. My fingers do not move over this instrument in the masterly manner which I see so many women's do. But then I have always supposed it to be my own fault—because I will not take the trouble of practising.

DARCY. No one admitted to the privilege of hearing you play could think anything wanting. We neither of us perform to strangers.

LADY CATHERINE. What are you talking of?

SCENE TWENTY-FIVE

Charlotte joins Elizabeth as the scene turns to the grove alongside Rosings Park. Darcy stands waiting for Elizabeth.

CHARLOTTE. Three times this week? Mr. Darcy has met you three times in the grove? My dear, Eliza, he must be in love with you...

ELIZABETH. Perhaps he has a difficulty of finding anything to do at Rosings. Gentlemen cannot always be within doors. I suppose he has a fondness for walking as I do.

CHARLOTTE. He certainly looks at you a great deal.

ELIZABETH. But goes on ten minutes altogether without opening his lips!

(Elizabeth walks alone.)

ELIZABETH. *(To the audience)* The first time:

(*She looks up to see Mr. Darcy. They stand awkwardly for a moment. And then walk together. The Ensemble sings THEIR GROVES OF SWEET MYRTLE*)

ENSEMBLE.

> THEIR GROVES O' SWEET MYRTLE
> LET FOREIGN LANDS RECKON,
> WHERE BRIGHT-BEAMING SUMMERS
> EXALT THE PERFUME;
> FAIR DEARER TO ME
> YON LONE GLEN O' GREEN BRECKAN,
> WI' THE BURN STEALING UNDER THE
> LANG, YELLOW BROOM.

ELIZABETH. *(To Mr. Darcy)* Mr. Bingley and his sisters are well, I hope, when you last left London?

MR. DARCY. Perfectly so, I thank you.

ELIZABETH. I think I have understood that Mr. Bingley has not much idea of ever returning to Netherfield again?

MR. DARCY. I should not be surprised if he were to give it up as soon as any eligible purchase offers.

ELIZABETH. *(To the audience.)* The second time: (*Elizabeth walks in the grove, sees Mr Darcy waiting, begins to turn. He catches up with her, offers his arm which she takes, hesitatingly. They are falling in love.*)

ENSEMBLE.

> FAIR DEARER TO ME
> ARE YON HUMBLE BROOM BOWERS
> WHERE THE BLUE-BELL AND GOWAN
> LURK, LOWLY, UNSEEN;
> FOR THERE, LIGHTLY TRIPPING,
> AMONG THE WILD FLOWERS,

A-LIST'NING THE LINNET,
AFT WANDERS MY LOVE.

MR. DARCY. Mr. Collins appears to be very fortunate in his choice of a wife.

ELIZABETH. I am not certain that I consider her marrying Mr. Collins as the wisest thing she ever did. Yet she seems perfectly happy and in a prudential light it is certainly a very good match for her.

MR. DARCY. It must be very agreeable for her to be settled within so easy a distance of her own family and friends.

ELIZABETH. Fifty miles? I should never have said Mrs. Collins was settled near her family.

MR. DARCY. It is a proof of your own attachment to Hertfordshire. Anything beyond the very neighbourhood of Longbourn, I suppose, would appear far?

ELIZABETH. *(To the audience.)* The third time: *(Elizabeth walks again, sees Mr. Darcy and this time, takes his arm without waiting to be invited.)*

ENSEMBLE.
THO' RICH IS THE BREEZE
IN THEIR GAY, SUNNY VALLEYS,
AND CAULD CALEDONIA'S
BLAST ON THE WAVE;
HE WANDERS AS FREE
AS THE WINDS OF HIS MOUNTAINS,
SAVE LOVE'S WILLING FETTERS
THE CHAINS OF HIS LOVE.

MR. DARCY. *(Teasingly.)* So this is the grove where you walk while the others are calling on Lady Catherine?

ELIZABETH. Yes, I feel quite beyond the reach of Lady Catherine's/

MR. DARCY. Curiosity!? *(She blushes as she realizes he agrees. He stumbles out his words.)*

MR. DARCY. I do hope you'll be comfortable there when you next return to Kent.

ELIZABETH. *(To the audience.)* Comfortable, at Rosings? When I return next to Kent? Whatever could he mean? *(He exits. She walks on.)*

SCENE TWENTY-SIX

The following morning after the evening at Rosings. Elizabeth turns, expecting to see Mr. Darcy, but sees instead that it is Fitzwilliam.

COLONEL FITZWILLIAM. I did not know you walked this way. Let me walk with you to the Parsonage.

ELIZABETH. Do you certainly leave Kent on Saturday?

COLONEL FITZWILLIAM. Yes — if Darcy does not put it off again. But I am at his disposal. He likes to have his own way very well. *(pause)* He has had some business in town today and will visit our ward but he will return tomorrow.

ELIZABETH. Your ward? Miss Darcy?

COLONEL FITZWILLIAM. I am joined with Mr. Darcy in the guardianship of his sister.

ELIZABETH. Are you indeed? And pray does your charge give you much trouble? Young ladies of her age are sometimes a little difficult to manage.

COLONEL FITZWILLIAM. I dare say she is one of the most tractable creatures in the world.

ELIZABETH. Indeed. She is a very great favourite with some ladies of my acquaintance, Mrs. Hurst and Miss Bingley. I think you said you know them.

COLONEL FITZWILLIAM. I know them a little. Their brother is a great friend of Darcy's.

ELIZABETH. Oh! yes. Mr. Darcy is uncommonly kind to Mr. Bingley.

COLONEL FITZWILLIAM. I have reason to think Bingley very much indebted to him.

ELIZABETH. What is it you mean?

COLONEL FITZWILLIAM. It is a circumstance which Darcy could not wish to be generally known, because if it were to get round to the lady's family, it would be an unpleasant thing.

ELIZABETH. You may depend upon my not mentioning it.

COLONEL FITZWILLIAM. He congratulated himself on having lately saved a friend from a most imprudent marriage. I understood there were some very strong objections against the lady.

ELIZABETH. I do not see what right Mr Darcy had to... *(Catching herself.)* Perhaps there was not much affection in the case.

COLONEL FITZWILLIAM. *(In jest.)* But then it would lessen of the honour of my cousin's triumph very sadly!

ELIZABETH. *(To the audience.)* Strong objections against the lady! Oh, Jane! *(To Fitzwilliam.)* I am afraid I will not be able to join her ladyship for tea.

FITZWILLIAM. Are you unwell, Miss Bennet?

ELIZABETH. A headache, nothing more. Pray excuse me. *(She runs on ahead to where she and Darcy have been walking in the grove. Fitzwilliam exits to find help.)*

SCENE TWENTY-SEVEN

ELIZABETH. Jane is all loveliness and goodness! *(Mr. Darcy enters.)*

MR. DARCY. I heard you are unwell and I've come to offer my assistance.

ELIZABETH. I am well. Thank you. I am sorry for your trouble.

MR. DARCY. It is no tro–/ *(He paces for a moment or two. Exhales, composes himself.)* In vain I have struggled. Despite all my endeavours to disregard your family's inferiority to mine. It will not do. My feelings will not be repressed. You must allow me to tell you how ardently I admire and love you.

ELIZABETH. *(Slowly intensifying.)* In such cases as this, it is, I believe, the established mode to express a sense of obligation for the sentiments avowed. If I could feel gratitude, I would now thank you. But I cannot — I have never desired your good opinion, and you have certainly bestowed it most unwillingly.

(He struggles to create the appearance of composure.)

MR. DARCY. And this is all the reply which I am to have the honour of expecting!? I might, perhaps, wish to be informed why, with so little endeavour at civility, I am thus rejected.

ELIZABETH. And I might as well enquire why with so evident a desire of insulting me, you chose to tell me that you liked me against your will, against your reason, and even against your character? But I have other provocations. You know I have. Do you think that any consideration would tempt me to accept the man who has been the means of ruining, perhaps for ever, the happiness of a most beloved sister? *(Pause.)* Can you deny that you have done it?

MR. DARCY. I have no wish of denying it. Towards him I have been kinder than towards myself.

ELIZABETH. Long before this, my opinion of you was decided in your behavior toward Mr. Wickham.

MR. DARCY. You take an eager interest in that gentleman's concerns...

ELIZABETH. Who that knows what his misfortunes have been, can help feeling an interest in him?

MR. DARCY. His misfortunes! Yes, his misfortunes have been great indeed.

ELIZABETH. You have reduced him to his present state of comparative poverty and yet you can treat the mention of his misfortune with contempt and ridicule.

MR. DARCY. And this is your opinion of me! I thank you for explaining it so fully. My faults, according to you, are heavy indeed! But perhaps these offenses might have been overlooked, had not your pride been hurt by my honest confession, had I, with greater policy, concealed my struggles, and flattered you into the belief of my being impelled by unqualified, unalloyed inclination; by reason, by reflection, by -- everything! But disguise of every sort is my abhorrence. I am not ashamed of the feelings I related. They were natural and just. Could you expect me to rejoice in the inferiority of your connections? To congratulate myself on the hope of relations, whose condition in life is so decidedly beneath my own?/

ELIZABETH. You are mistaken, Mr. Darcy, if you suppose that the mode of your declaration affected me in any other way than as it spared me the concern which I might have felt in refusing you, had you behaved in a more gentlemanlike manner.

(He bristles at this accusation.) You could not have made me the offer of your hand in any possible way that would have tempted me to accept it. From the very beginning — from the first moment of my acquaintance with you, your manners, your arrogance, your conceit... I had not known you a month before I felt that you were the last man in the world whom I could ever be prevailed on to marry.

MR. DARCY. You have said quite enough, madam. I perfectly comprehend your feelings. Forgive me for having taken up so much of your time, and accept my best wishes for your health and happiness.

INTERLUDE

ENSEMBLE sings THO YOU THINK BY THIS TO VEX ME. (The women may twirl, point and flick open and closed their fans in the "language of the fan" of the day.)

FEMALES.
>THO' YOU THINK BY THIS TO VEX ME
>LOVE NO MORE CAN GIVE ME PAIN.

MALES.
>VAINLY STRIVE NOT TO PERPLEX ME.
>YOU SHALL DUPE ME NE'ER AGAIN.

FEMALES.
>NOW YOUR FALSEHOOD IS REQUITED
>I'LL ENJOY A SINGLE LIFE!

MALES.
>HARK TO GLORY I'M INVITED
>BY THE CHEERFUL DRUM AND FIFE.

FEMALES.
>BY CONSENT THEN NOW WE SEVER.

MALES.

LOVE'S ALL NONSENSE;
FREEDOM'S SWEET!

FEMALES.

AND WE TAKE OUR LEAVE FOREVER

MALES.

NEVER MORE AGAIN TO MEET.

FEMALES.

NEVER MORE.

MALES.

NEVER MORE!

FEMALES.

NEVER MORE.

MALES.

NEVER MORE!

FEMALES.

I DON'T WISH, SIR, TO ALLURE YOU.
I DON'T WISH YOU STAY, NOT I.

MALES.

I'M QUITE HAPPY, I ASSURE YOU.
GLADLY I PRONOUNCE GOODBYE.
NOW I'M GONE, ADIEU FOREVER
GLADLY I PRONOUNCE GOODBYE.

FEMALES.

LA LA LA LA LA LA LA LA LA LA

MALES.

GLADLY I PRONOUNCE GOODBYE.

- INTERVAL -

ACT TWO
SCENE ONE

The following morning. Elizabeth walks again in the grove alongside Rosings Park as the Ensemble sings THEIR GROVES OF SWEET MYRTLE. Mr. Darcy enters with a note which he offers to her.

ENSEMBLE.
> THEIR GROVES O' SWEET MYRTLE
> LET FOREIGN LANDS RECKON,
> WHERE BRIGHT-BEAMING SUMMERS
> EXALT THE PERFUME;
> FAR DEARER TO ME
> YON LONE GLEN O' GREEN BRECKAN,
> WI' THE BURN STEALING UNDER
> THE LANG, YELLOW BROOM.
>
> FAR DEARER TO ME
> ARE YON HUMBLE BROOM BOWERS
> WHERE THE BLUE-BELL AND GOWAN
> LURK, LOWLY, UNSEEN;
> FOR THERE, LIGHTLY TRIPPING
> AMONG THE WILD FLOWERS,
> A-LIST'NING THE LINNET
> AFT WANDERS MY LOVE.

MR. DARCY. *(Looking slightly disheveled.)* I have been walking in the grove all morning in the hope of meeting you. Will you do me the honour of reading that letter?

(And then, with a slow, courteous bow, he exits. Elizabeth looks on after him as he goes. She then carefully opens the letter.)

ELIZABETH. *(Reading)* "Be not alarmed, madam, on receiving this letter. I shall not renew those sentiments which were last night so disgusting to you. Last night you laid two offenses to my charge. The first that I had detached Mr. Bingley from your sister, and the other, that I had, in defiance of honour and humanity, ruined the prospects of Mr Wickham." *(The Ensemble forms the lines of the dance at Netherfield. Jane dances with Mr. Bingley. The air of memory pervades the scene. Mr. Darcy enters and relates the contents of the letter Elizabeth clutches.)*

MR. DARCY. *(Reading.)* "As to the first, I had not been long in Hertfordshire, before I saw, in common with others, that Bingley preferred your elder sister to any other young woman in the country - a partiality beyond what I had ever witnessed in him before."

MRS. BENNET. *(To the audience.)* He seemed quite struck with Jane as she was going down the dance!

MR. DARCY. "But I remained convinced that while your sister received his attentions with pleasure, she did not invite them by any participation of sentiment."

CHARLOTTE. *(To the audience.)* In nine cases out of ten, a woman had better show more affection than she feels. He may never do more than like her, if she does not help him on.

MR. DARCY. "If I have been misled and have inflected pain on her, your resentment of me is not unreasonable."

JANE. *(To the audience.)* It is nothing in comparison of what I should feel in thinking ill of him or his sisters.

MR. DARCY. "I did not believe her to be indifferent because I wished it. However, my objections to the marriage were not merely my belief she was indifferent." *(Mary moves again to the piano to play ROBIN ADAIR. The Bennet family embarrasses themselves once again. Elizabeth blushes at the remembrance. As if a bad dream.)*

MARY.

    WHAT'S THIS DULL TOWN TO ME?
    ROBIN'S NOT NEAR

MR. DARCY. "The situation of your mother's family, though objectionable, was nothing in comparison to that total want of propriety so frequently, so almost uniformly betrayed by herself."

MRS. BENNET. Jane is soon to be engaged!

MARY.

    WHAT WAS'T I WISH'D TO SEE?
    WHAT WISH'D TO HEAR?

MR. DARCY. "By your three younger sisters."

MARY.

    WHERE'S ALL THE JOY AND MIRTH
    MADE THIS TOWN HEAVEN ON EARTH?

LYDIA. You promised!

MARY.

    OH, THEY'RE ALL FLED WITH THEE
    ROBIN ADAIR

MR. DARCY. "And occasionally even by your father."

MR. BENNET. Let the other young ladies have time to exhibit.

MR. DARCY. "From what passed that evening, my opinion of all parties was confirmed."

MRS. BENNET. So rich, and living but three miles from Longbourn!

MR. DARCY. "I acted to preserve my friend from what I esteemed a most unhappy connection. He left Netherfield for London, on the day following, as you, I am certain, remember. *(Jane meets with the Bingleys who are polite but very cold to her.)* Of your sister's being in town. I knew it myself, as did Miss Bingley; but her brother is even yet ignorant of it. If I have wounded your sister's feelings, it was unknowingly done. With respect to Mr. Wickham. Of what he has particularly accused me I am ignorant; but of the truth of what I shall relate, I can summon more than one witness of undoubted veracity. *(Mr. Wickham enters, looking entirely respectable.)* Mr. Wickham is the son of a very respectable man, who had for many years the management of the Pemberley estate. My father supported him at school, and afterwards at Cambridge and hoped the church would be his profession and intended to provide for him in it.

(Mr. Wickham contemplates taking orders.) My excellent father died about five years ago; in his will he desired Mr. Wickham should receive one thousand pounds and a place in the church as soon as it became vacant. *(He prefers women and cards and*

the stage business reflects this.) Within half a year, Mr. Wickham wrote to inform me he'd resolved against taking orders and intended to study law for which the interest of one thousand pounds would be very insufficient… I rather wished, than believed him to be sincere; but, at any rate, was perfectly ready to agree to his proposal.

(Mr. Wickham's eye falls upon a young lady passing. He follows.) I knew that Mr. Wickham ought not to be a clergyman, and accepted to give him three thousand pounds. All connection between us seemed now dissolved. *(Wickham enters in the company of Mrs. Younge. Drinking, gambling…)* But after three years he wrote again. In debt and demanding the living and place in the church my father had intended for him. You will hardly blame me for refusing to comply with his demands. I refused. How he lived I know not. But

I must now mention a circumstance which I would wish to forget myself, and which no obligation less than the present should induce me to unfold to any human being. *(Mr. Wickham and Mrs. Younge steal away with Georgiana Darcy.)* About a year ago, my sister, Georgiana Darcy, who is ten years my junior, was taken from school by her governess, Mrs. Younge, a woman in whose character we were most unhappily deceived. She was taken to Ramsgate and thither also went Mr. Wickham. *(Mr. Wickham charms Georgiana.)* He so recommended himself to Georgiana, whose affectionate heart retained a strong impression of his kindness to her as a child, that she was persuaded to believe herself in love, and to consent to an elopement. She was then but fifteen. *(Mr. Darcy joins his sister who runs to his side. He stands off with Mr. Wickham who tries to charm him.)* I am happy to add, that I owed the knowledge of it to herself. I joined them unexpectedly a day or two before the intended elopement, and Georgiana, unable to support the idea of grieving a brother whom she almost looks up to as a father, acknowledged the whole to me. You may imagine what I felt and how I acted. Regard for my sister prevented any public exposure. Mr. Wickham's chief object was unquestionably my sister's fortune, which is thirty thousand pounds; but I cannot help supposing that the hope of revenging himself on me was a strong inducement. His revenge would have been complete indeed. This, madam, is a faithful narrative of every event in which we have been concerned together; and if you do not absolutely reject it as false, you will, I hope, acquit me henceforth of cruelty towards Mr. Wickham. Last night, I was not then master enough of myself to know what could or ought to be revealed. For the truth of everything here related, I can appeal to the testimony of Colonel Fitzwilliam. You cannot be prevented by your abhorrence of me from confiding in my cousin; I shall endeavour to find some opportunity of putting this letter in your hands in the course of the morning. I will only add, God bless you — Fitzwilliam Darcy."

ELIZABETH. *(To the audience.)* This must be false! This cannot be! *(Pause.)* How despicably I have acted! I, who have prided myself on my discernment! How humiliating is this discovery! Yet, how just a humiliation! Had I been in love, I could not have been more wretchedly blind! But

vanity, not love, has been my folly. Pleased with the preference of one, and offended by the neglect of the other, on the very beginning of our acquaintance, I have driven reason away, where either were concerned. Till this moment I never knew myself. *(Pause.)* And Jane! How grievous is the thought that of a situation so desirable in every respect, so promising for happiness, Jane has been deprived, by the folly of her own family!
(Elizabeth leaves Hunsford.)
CHARLOTTE LUCAS. It seems but a day or two since you first came! and yet how many things have happened! How much you shall have to tell!
ELIZABETH. *(To the audience.)* How much I shall have to conceal. *(Ensemble resumes singing the THOU YOU THINK ... as the scene returns to Longbourn.)*
FEMALES.
>YOU HAVE CHANGED MY MIND,
>BELIEVE ME.

MALES.
>NO, I TOLD YOU SO BEFORE!

FEMALES.
>CAN YOU HAVE THE HEART TO LEAVE ME?

MALES.
>YES — I'LL NEVER SEE YOU MORE.

FEMALES.
>NEVER MORE?

MALES.
>NEVER MORE!

FEMALES.
>NEVER MORE?

MALES.
    NEVER MORE!
MALES/FEMALES.
    NO MORE? NO MORE! NO MORE! NO MORE?

SCENE TWO

At Longbourn; the sisters are bickering.

MR. BENNET. I am glad you are come back, Lizzy...
LYDIA. But papa! The officers are going to be encamped near Brighton!
KITTY. Please take us all there for the summer!
ELIZABETH. *(Removing her bonnet.)* Good Heavens! Brighton, and a whole camp full of soldiers. Father...
MR. BENNET. I've not the smallest intention of yielding.
LYDIA. I dare say it would hardly cost anything at all. Mamma would like to go too of all things!
MRS. BENNET. I am sure I cried for two days together when Colonel Miller's regiment went away. I thought I should have broken my heart.
LYDIA. I am sure the officers' leaving us shall break mine!
MRS. BENNET. If one could but go to Brighton!
KITTY. Oh, yes! But papa is so disagreeable.
LYDIA. A little sea-bathing would set me up forever! Oh, but Lizzy! Now I have got some news for you! There is no danger of Wickham's marrying Mary King. She is gone to her uncle at Liverpool: gone to stay. Wickham is safe!

ELIZABETH. *(To the audience.)* Mary King is safe!

JANE. But I hope there is no strong attachment on either side. *(Jane reads the letter from Mr. Darcy which Elizabeth has pressed into her hand.)*

LYDIA. I am sure there is not on his. Who could care about such a nasty little freckled thing?! *(All except Jane and Lizzy follow after Mr. Bennet who attempts to seek safety in his study.)*

JANE. Poor Mr. Darcy! Dear Lizzy, only consider what he must have suffered. Such a disappointment! and having to relate such a thing of his sister! It is really too distressing. I am sure you must feel it so.

ELIZABETH. You do not blame me, however, for refusing him?

JANE. Blame you! Oh, no. *(Pause.)* But Wickham so very bad!? It is almost past belief. There is such an expression of goodness in his countenance!

ELIZABETH. One has got all the goodness, and the other all the appearance of it.

JANE. I never thought Mr. Darcy so deficient in his appearance as you used to do.

ELIZABETH. And yet I meant to be uncommonly clever in taking so decided a dislike to him, without any reason. *(Pause.)* Jane. I want to be told whether I ought to make our family and acquaintances understand Wickham's character.

JANE. Surely there can be no occasion for exposing him so dreadfully. What is your opinion?

ELIZABETH. Mr. Darcy has not authorised me to make his communication public. Wickham will soon be gone. At present I will say nothing about it.

(Jane nods and walks on alone. Mrs. Bennet corners Elizabeth.)

MRS. BENNET. Well, Lizzy I do not suppose there's the least chance in the world of her ever getting Mr. Bingley now?!

ELIZABETH. I do not believe he will ever return to Netherfield.

MRS. BENNET. Well, my comfort is, Jane will die of a broken heart; and then he will be sorry for what he has done! *(Lydia rushes in clutching a letter.)*

LYDIA. My very particular friend Mrs. Forster has invited me to go with her and the Colonel to Brighton!

KITTY. I cannot see why Mrs. Forster should not ask me as well as Lydia?! I have just as much right to be asked as she!

ELIZABETH. Oh, Father, do not let Lydia go to Brighton where the temptations must be greater than at home. *(Kitty listens in.)*

MR. BENNET. Now, now, Elizabeth... Lydia will never be easy until she has exposed herself in some public place or other.

ELIZABETH. Excuse me, for I must speak plainly. If you, my dear father, will not take the trouble of checking her exuberant spirits, she will, at sixteen, be the most determined flirt that ever made herself or her family ridiculous.

MR. BENNET. Do not make yourself uneasy, my love. Wherever you and Jane are known, you will be respected and valued. Colonel Forster is a sensible man, and will keep her out of any real mischief; and she is luckily too poor to be an object of prey to anybody.

LYDIA. I'll write long letters...!

MARY. Her letters will be long - long expected and always very short!

KITTY. Lydia will go to to Brighton! And Lizzy to the lakes! What a miserable summer I shall have! *(She runs off in tears. Elizabeth reads a letter.)*

ELIZABETH. No, not the lakes… *(Sighs, hands letter to Mary who reads it.)*

MARY. *(Reading.)* "Dearest Eliza, Mr. Gardiner will be prevented by business this summer to go so far as to the Lakes. We will be able to go no farther than Derbyshire. First to Lambton, the scene of my former residence which is within five miles of Pemberely..." Pemberley? That big house? Mr. Darcy's Pemberley?

SCENE THREE

The Bennets exit. Elizabeth joins her uncle and aunt at the entrance to Pemberley.

MR. GARDINER. It would have been a shame not to see a place of which you have heard so much!

MRS. GARDINER. Wickham passed all his youth here, you know....

ELIZABETH. I'm tired; after going over so many great houses, I really have no pleasure in fine carpets or satin curtains/

MRS. GARDINER. If it were merely a fine house, I should not care about it myself; but the grounds are delightful.

MR. GARDINER. They have some of the finest woods in the country.

ELIZABETH. Are we certain the owners are away for the summer? *(Elizabeth surveys the house and gardens with delight.)* I've never seen a place for which nature has done more. *(To the audience.)* To be mistress of Pemberley might have been something!

(They enter the house, escorted by the Housekeeper, Mrs. Reynolds.)

ELIZABETH. The rooms are lofty and handsome and the furniture neither gaudy nor uselessly fine. *(To the audience.)* And of this place I might have been mistress!

MRS. REYNOLDS. We expect Mr. Darcy tomorrow, with a large party of friends.

(Stopping to view some miniatures, portraits or busts of the family.)

MRS. GARDINER. How do you like it, Elizabeth?

MRS. REYNOLDS. That is Mr. Wickham. But he has turned out very wild.

(Mrs. Gardiner smiles but Elizabeth cannot join her.)

MRS. REYNOLDS. And that, is my master — Mr. Darcy.

MRS. GARDINER. It is a handsome face. But, Lizzy, you can tell us whether it is like or not.

MRS. REYNOLDS. Does that young lady know Mr. Darcy?

ELIZABETH. A little...

MRS. REYNOLDS. And do not you think him a very handsome gentleman, ma'am?

ELIZABETH. Yes, very handsome.

MRS. GARDINER. And is Miss Darcy as handsome as her brother?

MRS. REYNOLDS. Oh! yes — the handsomest young lady that ever was seen; and so accomplished! She plays and sings all day long. In the next room is a new instrument just come down for her — a present from my master; she comes here tomorrow with him.

MR. GARDINER. Is your master much at Pemberley in the course of the year?

MRS. REYNOLDS. Not so much as I could wish.

MR. GARDINER. If your master would marry, you might see more of him.

MRS. REYNOLDS. Yes, sir; but I do not know who is good enough for him. I have never known a cross word and I have known him ever since he was four years old.

ELIZABETH. *(To the audience)* Can this be Mr. Darcy?

MRS. GARDINER. His father was an excellent man...

MRS. REYNOLDS. Yes, ma'am, that he was indeed; and his son will be just like him. Some people call him proud; but I am sure I never saw anything of it. To my fancy, it is only because he does not rattle away like other young men.

MRS. GARDINER. This fine account of him is not quite consistent with his behaviour to our poor friend, Mr. Wickham.

ELIZABETH. Perhaps we might be deceived… *(Mr. and Mrs. Gardiner walk on. Mr. Darcy enters from the stables. He has just arrived. He walks with ease, delighted to be home, looking positively natural and relaxed on his own grounds. Their eyes meet. They blush. She looks down.)*

MR. DARCY. Miss Bennet. Your family, they are well?

ELIZABETH. Yes, thank you.

MR. DARCY. And are you long in Derbyshire?

ELIZABETH. A few weeks. We are staying in Lambton, at the Inn. *(He suddenly bows and takes his leave. Elizabeth is distraught, embarrassed, wishes to run off. The Ensemble (as Pemberley gardeners, maids etc) sing Henry Purcell's I ATTEMPT FROM LOVE'S SICKNESS TO FLY IN VAIN)*

ELIZABETH. Our coming here was the most ill-judged thing in the world! How it must appear to him! Oh! Why did we come? We must leave at once! *(She looks about to find Mr. and Mrs. Gardiner.)*

ELIZABETH.

    I ATTEMPT FROM LOVE'S SICKNESS
    TO FLY IN VAIN
    SINCE I AM MYSELF, MY OWN FEVER
    SINCE I AM MYSELF, MY OWN FEVER
    AND PAIN

ENSEMBLE.

    NO MORE NOW
    NO MORE NOW

FOND HEART
WITH PRIDE NO MORE SWELL
THOU CANST NOT RAISE FORCES
THOU CANST NOT RAISE FORCES
ENOUGH TO REBEL

(Mr. Darcy returns, more formally dressed. Elizabeth stands opposite Mr. Darcy. Both are at a loss for words until Mr. and Mrs. Gardiner return to join them.)

MR. DARCY. Would you do me the honour of introducing me to your friends? *(Elizabeth smiles in relief at this and introductions are made.)*

ELIZABETH. Mr. Darcy, my uncle, Mr. Gardiner and his wife. *(They bow/nod.)*

MRS. GARDINER. *(To explain their presence.)* We understood from your housekeeper that you were not immediately expected in the country.

MR. DARCY. It's true. Business with my steward occasioned my coming before the rest of the party... *(To Elizabeth.)* They will join me early tomorrow: Mr. Bingley and his sisters. There is also one other person in the party who more particularly wishes to be known to you. My sister. Will you allow me to introduce my sister to you during your stay at Lambton? *(She nods and smiles as Mr. Darcy is approached by the Head Gardener or his Steward. He excuses himself and exits.)*

MRS. GARDINER. How came you to tell me that he was so disagreeable?

MR. GARDINER. He is perfectly well behaved, polite, and unassuming.

ELIZABETH. I cannot account for it. I have never seen him so pleasant as this morning.

MRS. GARDINER. From what we have seen of him, I really should not have thought that he could have been so cruel to poor Wickham.

ELIZABETH. His character is by no means so faulty, nor Wickham's so amiable as we had first considered. Oh Aunt, I have much I must tell you...

SCENE FOUR

The Inn at Lambton the following morning. Mr. Darcy enters with Mr. Bingley and his sister, Miss Georgiana Darcy. Introductions are made. She and Elizabeth like one another immediately and talk quietly together. Elizabeth helps ease Miss Darcy out of her shyness; by the end of the song they are fully in each other's confidence.

MR. DARCY. My sister, Miss Darcy. Miss Bennet. And Mr. Bingley!

MR. BINGLEY. We have not met since the 26th of November when we were all dancing together at Netherfield!

ELIZABETH. Your memory is so exact!
(Mr. Darcy whispers to his sister and she musters up the courage to make the invitation.)
MISS DARCY. We invite you to dine at Pemberley.
(Music starts for WHAT SHALL I DO TO SHOW HOW MUCH I LOVE HER? As the scene shifts to Pemberley.

The Bingley sisters enter. Miss Darcy plays the piano and Elizabeth turns the pages while observing Mr. Darcy. He is removed from the action but still observes Elizabeth as she interacts with his sister. He sings in "an aside."

MR. DARCY.

 WHAT SHALL I DO
 TO SHOW HOW MUCH I LOVE HER?
 THOUGHTS THAT OPPRESS ME
 OH, HOW CAN I TELL?

 WILL MY SOFT PASSION
 BE ABLE TO MOVE HER?
 LANGUAGE IS WANTING
 WHEN LOVING SO WELL.

MISS DARCY. *(Looking to Mr. Darcy.)* Yes. He is certainly a good brother. There isn't anything in the world he wouldn't do for me.

MRS. HURST. Pray, Miss Eliza, have all the officers been removed from Meryton? All those soldiers… It must be a great loss to *your* family! *(Miss Darcy stops playing the piano. Mr. Darcy looks helplessly for one brief moment at Elizabeth who, understanding the scandal which he, Elizabeth and his sister wish to keep secret, draws close to Miss Darcy who thereby regains her composure.)*

MR. DARCY.

 CAN SIGHS AND TEARS,
 IN THE SILENCE, BETOKEN
 HALF THE DISTRESS
 THIS FOND BOSOM MUST KNOW?
 OR WILL SHE MELT

WHEN A TRUE HEART IS BROKEN,
WEEPING, TOO LATE,
O'ER HER LOST LOVER'S WOE.

CAROLINE BINGLEY. *(Interrupting his reverie.)* How very ill Eliza Bennet looks this morning, Mr. Darcy. I recollect your once saying of Miss Eliza: "She a beauty! I should as soon call her mother a wit."

MR. DARCY. Yes, but that was only when I first saw her. It is many months since I have considered her one of the handsomest women of my acquaintance.

SCENE FIVE

The scene returns again to the Inn at Lambton where Elizabeth sits writing/reading, the Gardiners are preparing to go out.

ENSEMBLE.
WHAT SHALL I DO
TO SHOW HOW MUCH I LOVE HER?
THOUGHTS THAT OPPRESS ME
OH, HOW CAN I TELL?
WILL MY SOFT PASSION
BE ABLE TO MOVE HER?
LANGUAGE IS WANTING
WHEN LOVING - SO - WELL.

(A servant brings Elizabeth two letters. Mr. and Mrs. Gardiner prepare to leave.)

ELIZABETH. Oh, letters from Jane! Two at once?

MR. AND MRS. GARDINER. We'll leave you to enjoy them in quiet. *(They exit.)*

ELIZABETH. *(Reading)* "Since writing the above, dearest Lizzy, something has occurred of a most serious nature. An express came at twelve last night, just as we were all gone to bed, from Colonel Forster, to inform us that Lydia has gone off to Scotland with Wickham! Imagine our surprise. To Kitty, however, it does not seem so wholly unexpected…" *(Elizabeth hurriedly opens the second letter. Jane enters.)*

JANE. *(Reciting the letter.)* Dearest Lizzy, I have bad news for you, and it cannot be delayed. Imprudent as the marriage between Mr. Wickham and our poor Lydia would be, we are now anxious to be assured that sit has taken place. There is reason to fear they are not gone to Scotland. Can I suppose her so lost as to consent to live with him on any terms other than marriage? Father is going to London with Colonel Forster instantly, to try to discover her.

ELIZABETH. Oh! where, where is my uncle? *(Mr. Darcy appears, startled.)* I beg your pardon, but I must leave you. I must find Mr. Gardiner this moment!

MR. DARCY. Let me, or let the servant go after Mr. and Mrs. Gardiner. You are not well. *(To a servant passing.)* Fetch your master and mistress instantly. *(To Lizzy.)* Is there nothing you could take? A glass of wine? You are very ill.

ELIZABETH. No, I thank you. I am quite well; I am only distressed by some dreadful news which I have just received from Longbourn. *(She bursts into tears.)* I have just had a letter from Jane, with such dreadful news. It cannot be concealed from anyone. My younger sister has left all her friends — has eloped; has thrown herself into the power of — of Mr. Wickham. They are gone off together from Brighton. You know him too well to doubt the rest. She has no money, no connections, nothing that can tempt him to - she is lost for ever. *(Pause.)* When I consider that I might have prevented it! I who knew what he was. Had I but explained some part of it only — some part of what I learnt, to my own family! Had his character been known… But it is all — all too late now.

MR. DARCY. I am grieved indeed. But is it certain — absolutely certain?

ELIZABETH. Oh, yes! They left Brighton together on Sunday night, and were traced almost to London, but not beyond; they are certainly not gone to Scotland to marry!

MR. DARCY. And what has been done, what has been attempted, to recover her?

ELIZABETH. My father is gone to London, and Jane has written to beg my uncle's immediate assistance; and we shall be off, I hope, in half-an-hour. But nothing can be done — How is such a man to be worked on? How are they even to be discovered? I have not the smallest hope.

MR. DARCY. *(After a long, silent pause.)* I am afraid you have been long desiring my absence. This unfortunate affair will, I fear, prevent my sister's having the pleasure of seeing you again at Pemberley today.

ELIZABETH. Oh, yes. Be so kind as to apologise for us to Miss Darcy. Say that urgent business calls us home immediately. Conceal the unhappy truth as long as it is possible, I know it cannot be long. *(With only one serious, parting look, he exits. Elizabeth addresses the audience.)* We shall never see each other again.

SCENE SIX

Mr. and Mrs. Gardiner enter in great alarm. Mr. Gardiner exits. The scene shifts to both Longbourn and the chaos of London simultaneously; Elizabeth returns home to find Jane clutching a letter Kitty has been hiding; Mrs. Bennet has collapsed in a chair; in London, Mr. Gardiner joins Mr. Bennet and Colonel Forster in his search for Lydia.

ELIZABETH. Oh Jane, you look pale. How much you must have gone through!

JANE. I am perfectly well.

(Lydia and Wickham are in London. Lydia tries to write while there is much drinking and merriment around her. Wickham laughs, sings, flirts with other women, toasts with Mrs. Younge etc. Kitty snatches the letter back from Jane and reads it as Lydia writes it.)

KITTY. *(Reading, full of self importance to finally have some attention.)* "Dear Kitty, I cannot help laughing at your surprise as soon as I am missed. I am going to Gretna

Green, and if you cannot guess with who, I shall think you a simpleton…" But, of course, I could guess who! Lydia has eloped with Mr. Wickham! Gone to Gretna Green! *(Enviously.)* How romantic. Lydia, a married woman!
JANE. If they are indeed married…
ELIZABETH. Oh! thoughtless, thoughtless Lydia!
(The Ensemble gathers offering different information, voices, gossip, news overlapping.)
MARY. This is a most unfortunate affair, and will probably be much talked of. But we must stem the tide of malice, and pour into the wounded bosoms of each other the balm of sisterly consolation.
ENSEMBLE. *(Lines divided/doubled etc.)* Mr. Wickham! He's the wickedest young man in the world! He's in debt to every tradesman in Meryton. I always distrusted the appearance of his goodness. He's left gaming debts behind him! Why did the Forsters let her out of their sight? Will Mr. Bennet fight Wickham? Then he will be killed! The estate is entailed on the cousin, Mr. Collins....
MR. COLLINS. *(To the audience.)* The death of their daughter would have been a blessing in comparison to this!
MR. GARDINER. *(To the audience.)* She has been found! They are not married.
MR. BENNET. *(Returning home. The girls run to his side.)* No officer is *ever* to enter into my house again! *(Walks off on his own.)*
KITTY. Oh Father.... *(Runs off crying.)*
ENSEMBLE. They must marry! But to such a man! With such a husband her misery is certain.

(Mrs. Hill approaches Jane and Elizabeth.)
MRS. HILL. I beg your pardon, madam, for interrupting you, but I was in hopes you might have got some good news from town, so I took the liberty of coming to ask.

JANE. What do you mean, Hill? We've heard nothing from town.

MRS. HILL. Dear madam, there is an express come for master from Mr. Gardiner! *(Mr. Bennet enters with the letter. The girls run to him, read the letter.)*

MR. GARDINER. *(Announcing to the audience.)* It's all arranged. She will be married from our house in London…
(Elizabeth and Jane comfort their father.)

ENSEMBLE. No man in his senses would marry the girl! Wickham's a fool if he takes her for less than ten thousand pounds. Ten thousand pounds? That young man's marrying her is a patched-up business, at the expense of her father and uncles. Heaven forbid!

MR. BENNET. *(To Elizabeth and Jane.)* How am I ever to repay your uncle?! *(They continue reading.)*

MR. GARDINER *(To the audience.)* Mr. Wickham intends to go into the regulars. They will stop at Longbourn on their way North to/

MRS. BENNET. Newcastle! Such a distance as that! Oh, but Lydia is to be married! At sixteen! My dear, dear Lydia! This is delightful indeed! I shall see her again! My good, kind brother! I knew how it would be — I knew he would manage everything. Mrs. Wickham! How well it sounds! But the clothes, the wedding clothes! They should be ordered immediately! *(She exits as…)*

SCENE SEVEN

Lydia, loud, giggling and Mr. Wickham, charming as usual, arrive at Longbourn. Mr. Wickham talks with Mr. Bennet. Elizabeth enters last.

LYDIA. Well, mamma. Is not my husband a charming man? I am sure my sisters must all envy me. They must all go to Brighton. That is the place to get husbands.

JANE. No thank you. I do not particularly like your way of getting husbands.

LYDIA. Lizzy, I never gave you an account of my wedding. You were not by, when I told mamma and the others all about it. Are not you curious to hear?

ELIZABETH. Not really. I think there cannot be too little said on the subject.

LYDIA. Well, it was the moment when my uncle was to give me away; luckily, he came back again in time. However, I recollected afterwards that Mr. Darcy might have done as well to step in for Father and give me away…/

ELIZABETH. Mr. Darcy!?

LYDIA. Oh, yes! Oh! I quite forgot! I ought not to have said a word about it. I promised them so faithfully! It was to be such a secret! *(They move to exit. Jane steps ahead as is usual for the oldest daughter but Lydia stops her.)*

Ah! Jane, I take your place now, because I am a married woman.

(Elizabeth and Mr. Bennet observe Mr. Wickham.)

MR. BENNET. He is as fine a fellow as ever I saw. He simpers, and smirks, and makes love to us all.

ELIZABETH. *(To the audience.)* Mr. Darcy has done all this for a girl whom he neither regards nor esteems? *(She places her hand on her heart in realization of the truth.)* He has done it for me. *(She walks. Mr. Wickham joins her.)*

MR. WICKHAM. I am afraid I interrupt your solitary ramble, my dear sister.

ELIZABETH. You certainly do, but it does not follow that the interruption must be unwelcome.

MR. WICKHAM. I should be sorry, indeed, if it were. We were always good friends *(Pause.)* So, my dear sister, I find, from our uncle and aunt, that you have actually seen Pemberley.

ELIZABETH. I have indeed.

MR. WICKHAM. And you saw the old housekeeper, I suppose? Poor Reynolds, she was always very fond of me.

ELIZABETH. Yes. She said that you were gone into the army, and she was afraid you had — not turned out well. *(Pause.)* At such a distance as that, you know, things are strangely misrepresented.

MR. WICKHAM. Undoubtedly. I understood from the Gardiners that you had seen Mr. Darcy in Lambton.

ELIZABETH. Yes, he introduced us to his sister.

MR. WICKHAM. And do you like her?

ELIZABETH. Very much.

MR. WICKHAM. I have heard, indeed, that she is uncommonly improved within this year or two. When I last saw her, she was not very promising. I hope she will turn out well.

ELIZABETH. I dare say she will; she has got over the most trying age.

MR. WICKHAM. Did you go by the parish of Kympton? I mention it because it is the living which I ought to have had. A most delightful place! Excellent parsonage-house! It would have suited me in every respect.

ELIZABETH. How should you have liked making sermons?

MR. WICKHAM. Exceedingly well.

ELIZABETH. I have heard the living, the parsonage was left you conditionally only.

MR. WICKHAM. You have! Yes, I told you so from the first, you may remember.

ELIZABETH. I did hear, too, that there was a time when sermon-making was not so palatable to you as it seems to be at present.

MR. WICKHAM. You did! You may remember what I told you on that point, when first we talked of it.

ELIZABETH. Come, Mr. Wickham, we are brother and sister, you know. Do not let us quarrel about the past. *(She holds out her hand which he kisses half not knowing where to look as he has so clearly been seen through. The Bennet family enters to wave him and Lydia goodbye.)*

SCENE EIGHT

The Ensemble (as guests, servants, villagers) gather again to gossip. A servant hands Mrs. Bennet a note and then starts the gossip on its way.

ENSEMBLE. Mr. Bingley is returning to Netherfield? Mr. Bingley? Netherfield? Yes. We've orders to prepare for his arrival. He's coming to shoot for several weeks.

MRS. BENNET. My dear Mr. Bennet, when Mr. Bingley comes you will invite him, when he has shot all of his birds, to come and shoot as many birds as he pleases here at Longbourn.

MR. BENNET. No, no. He knows where we live. I will not be running after my neighbours every time they go away and come back again.

MRS. BENNET. Well, that shan't prevent my asking him to dine here. I am determined. We must have Mrs. Long and the Gouldings soon so... that will make thirteen, oh no! *(She exits re-counting, planning.)*

JANE. Mr. Bingley invited here? My dear Lizzy, you cannot think me so weak, as to be in danger now?

ELIZABETH. I think you are in very great danger of making him as much in love with you as ever.

SCENE NINE

A large party assembles at Longbourn.

KITTY. It's Mr. Bingley, mamma! And there is a gentleman with him. That Mr. What's-his-name. That tall, proud man.

MRS. BENNET. Mr. Darcy!?

Any friend of Mr. Bingley's will always be welcome here, to be sure; but else I must say that I hate the very sight of him. *(A servant presents Mr. Darcy and Mr. Bingley.)* It is a long time, Mr. Bingley, since you went away. *(Mr. Darcy stares out at the grounds until Mr. Bennet approaches him. Mr. Darcy notes the book in Mr. Bennet's hands and they discuss it quietly. Mr. Bingley stands opposite Jane.)*

ELIZABETH. *(To the audience.)* Why, if he came only to be silent and indifferent to me did he come at all? How could I ever be foolish enough to expect a renewal of his love? *(Mrs. Bennet winks repeatedly at Kitty while the rest of the family sits around awkwardly.)*

KITTY. What is the matter mamma? What do you keep winking at me for? What am I to do?

MRS. BENNET. Nothing child, nothing. I did not wink at you! Lizzy, my dear, I want to speak with you. Kitty, you as well. *(The Bennet family exits leaving Jane and Mr. Bingley alone. Elizabeth is also alone to sing I HAVE A SILENT SORROW HERE by Georgiana Cavendish.*

During the course of the song, Mr. Bingley leans toward Jane, whispers to her his proposal of marriage; she nods her acceptance.)

ELIZABETH.

> I HAVE A SILENT SORROW HERE,
> A GRIEF I'LL NE'ER IMPART;
> IT BREATHES NO SIGH
> IT SHEDS NO TEAR
> BUT IT CONSUMES MY HEART!

(Mr. Bingley moves to speak with Mr. Bennet who is ready to go out shooting with Mr. Darcy. Elizabeth dries her eyes and greets Jane; she is genuinely happy for her.)

JANE. How shall I bear so much happiness! Oh! Lizzy! If I could but see you as happy! If there were but such another man for you!

ELIZABETH. Till I have your goodness, I never can have your happiness. *(To the audience.)* Perhaps, if I have very good luck, I may meet with another Mr. Collins in time. *(The Ensemble celebrates the good news, laughing, toasting. Mrs. Bennet tells Mrs. Philips who tells someone else…The scene is similar to the opening tableaux with the ensemble singing THE JOYS OF THE COUNTRY. Mr. Bingley, Mr. Darcy and Mr. Bennet go shooting together.)*

ENSEMBLE. If you were to give me forty such men, I never could be so happy as Jane Bennet! She will be a very happy woman indeed. They are both so complying, that nothing will ever be resolved on… So easy, that every servant will cheat cheat them! And so generous, they will always exceed their income. Exceed their income!

What are you talking of? Why, he has four or five
thousand a year, very likely more. The Bennets are the
luckiest family in the world!

ENSEMBLE.
> OH THE MOUNTAINS AND VALLEYS
> AND BUSHES
> THE PIGS AND THE SCREECH OWLS
> AND THRUSHES
> LET BUCKS AND LET BLOODS
> TO PRAISE LONDON AGREE
> OH THE JOYS OF THE COUNTRY,
> MY JEWEL. FOR ME (repeat)

SCENE TEN

*Morning at Longbourn. If possible, Mary carries on
practicing THE JOYS OF THE COUNTRY until:*

KITTY. We've a visitor!

MARY. It's too early in the
morning for visitors.
KITTY. It's not a carriage
I've seen before.
JANE. The horses are
post.
ELIZABETH. It is Lady
Catherine de Bourgh!
(The girls scramble to

receive Lady Catherine who enters ungraciously. Looks around disdainfully.)
LADY CATHERINE. *(To Elizabeth)* I hope you are well, Miss Bennet. That lady, I suppose, is your mother.
ELIZABETH. She is.
LADY CATHERINE. And these, your sisters. This must be a most inconvenient sitting-room for the evening in summer: the windows are full west.
MRS. BENNET. But I assure you we never sit here after/
LADY CATHERINE. Miss Bennet, there is a prettyish kind of a little wilderness on one side of your lawn. I should be glad to take a turn in it, if you will favour me with your company.
MRS. BENNET. Go, my dear and show her ladyship about the different walks. I think she will be pleased with the hermitage. *(The Ensemble sings as Elizabeth and Lady Catherine move outside.)*
ENSEMBLE.

> HOW SWEET IN THE WOODLANDS
> WITH FLEET, HOUND AND HORN
> TO WAKEN SHRILL ECHO
> AND TASTE THE FRESH MORN
>
> BUT HARD IS THE CHANCE
> MY FOND HEART MUST PURSUE
> FOR DAPHNE, FAIR DAPHNE
> IS LOST TO MY VIEW
> SHE'S LOST, FAIR DAPHNE
> IS LOST TO MY VIEW

LADY CATHERINE. You can be at no loss, Miss Bennet, to understand the reason of my journey hither. Your own heart, your own conscience, must tell you why I have come.

ELIZABETH. Indeed, Madam. I am not at all able to account for the honour of seeing you here so early/

LADY CATHERINE. Miss Bennet you ought to know, that I am not to be trifled with. But however insincere you may choose to be, you shall not find me so. My character has ever been celebrated for its sincerity and frankness. A report of a most alarming nature reached me two days ago. I was told that not only your sister was on the point of being most advantageously married, but that you, that Miss Elizabeth Bennet, would, in all likelihood, be soon afterwards united to my nephew, Mr. Darcy.

ELIZABETH. If you believed it impossible, I wonder you took the trouble of coming so far. What could your ladyship propose by it?

LADY CATHERINE. At once to insist upon having such a report universally contradicted.

ELIZABETH. Your coming to Longbourn will be rather a confirmation of it; if, indeed, such a report exists.

LADY CATHERINE. This is not to be borne. Miss Bennet, I insist on being satisfied. Has he, has my nephew, made you an offer of marriage?

ELIZABETH. Your ladyship has declared it to be impossible. If I has, I shall be the last person to confess it.

LADY CATHERINE. I am the nearest relation he has in the world, and am entitled to know all his dearest concerns!

ELIZABETH. But you are not entitled to know mine.

LADY CATHERINE. Mr. Darcy is engaged to my daughter. They have been intended for each other from their infancy....

ELIZABETH. Then you can have no reason to suppose he will make an offer to me.

LADY CATHERINE. Obstinate, headstrong girl! I am ashamed of you! Is this your gratitude for my attentions to you last spring? I am not in the habit of brooking disappointment/

ELIZABETH. That will make your ladyship's situation at present more pitiable; but it will have no effect on me.

LADY CATHERINE. I will not be interrupted. Hear me in silence. They are destined for each other and what is to divide them? The upstart pretensions of a young woman without family, connections, or fortune. This is not to be endured! If you were sensible of your own good, you would not wish to quit the sphere in which you have been brought up.

ELIZABETH. In marrying your nephew, I should not consider myself as quitting that sphere. He is a gentleman; I am a gentleman's daughter; so far we are equal.

LADY CATHERINE. True. You are a gentleman's daughter. But who was your mother? Who are your uncles and aunts? Do not imagine me ignorant of their condition.

ELIZABETH. Whatever my connections may be, if your nephew does not object to them, they can be nothing to you.

LADY CATHERINE. Tell me once for all, are you engaged to him?

ELIZABETH. *(pause)* I am not.

LADY CATHERINE. And will you promise me, never to enter into such an engagement?

ELIZABETH. I will make no promise of the kind. *(She turns to leave.)*

LADY CATHERINE. Not so hasty, if you please. I am no stranger to the particulars of your youngest sister's infamous elopement. I know it all. And is such a girl to be my nephew's sister? Is her husband, to be his brother? Heaven and earth! Are the shades of Pemberley to be thus polluted?

ELIZABETH. You have insulted me in every possible method. I must beg to return to the house.

LADY CATHERINE. You are then resolved to have him?

ELIZABETH. I have said no such thing. I am only resolved to act in that manner, which will, in my own opinion, constitute my happiness, without reference to you, or to any person so wholly unconnected with me.

LADY CATHERINE. I take no leave of you, Miss Bennet. I send no compliments to your mother. You deserve no such attention. I am most seriously displeased. *(Lady Catherine exits. Ensemble sings THOU YOU THINK BY THIS TO VEX ME.)*

ENSEMBLE.

> THO' YOU THINK BY THIS TO VEX ME
> LOVE NO MORE CAN GIVE ME PAIN.
> VAINLY STRIVE NOT TO PERPLEX ME.
> YOU SHALL DUPE ME NE'ER AGAIN.
> NOW YOUR FALSEHOOD IS REQUITED
> I'LL ENJOY A SINGLE LIFE!

SCENE ELEVEN

Mrs. Bennet sees Mr. Bingley and Mr. Darcy arrive at Longbourn. Once again, the sisters hurriedly straighten up where they've been sitting.

MRS. BENNET. Good gracious! If that disagreeable Mr. Darcy is not coming here again with our dear Bingley! So he may not be in Bingley's way, Lizzy you must/
(The men enter.) Elizabeth. You must walk out with Mr. Darcy to Oakham Mount this morning…with Kitty.
MR. BINGLEY. *(Winking at Kitty.)* I am sure Oakham Mount will be too much for Kitty. Won't it, Kitty?
KITTY. The winking again? The winking again?! Oh! Oh! *(Looking at her sister Elizabeth and Mr. Darcy.)* Yes! I'd much rather stay at home. *(Elizabeth walks with Mr. Darcy; they walk ahead of Mr. Bingley and Jane who trail behind them.)*
ELIZABETH. Mr. Darcy, I have been most anxious to acknowledge to you how grateful I feel for what I suspect you have done for my family. Lydia's thoughtlessness betrayed it to me.
MR. DARCY. If you will thank me, let it be for yourself alone. Your family owe me nothing. Much as I respect your family, I thought only of you. *(pause)* You are too generous to trifle with me. If your feelings are still what they were last April, tell me so at once. My affections and wishes are unchanged, but one word from you will silence me on this subject for ever.

ELIZABETH. My feelings are not at all what they were last April. They are quite different. *(They both smile broadly but hardly dare look at one another.)*
MR. DARCY. We're indebted, you know, to my Aunt's curiosity. Her visit to you taught me to hope as I had scarcely ever allowed myself to hope before. I knew enough of your disposition to be certain that, had you been absolutely decided against me, you would have acknowledged it to Lady Catherine, frankly and openly.
ELIZABETH. Yes, you know enough of my frankness to believe me capable of that. After abusing you so abominably to your face, I could have no scruple in abusing you to all your relations.
MR. DARCY. What did you say of me that I did not deserve? The recollection of what I then said, of my conduct, my manners, my expressions during the whole of it, is now, and has been many months, inexpressibly painful to me. Your reproof I shall never forget: "Had you behaved in a more gentlemanlike manner." Those were your words. You know not, you can scarcely conceive, how they have tortured me; though it was some time, I confess, before I was reasonable enough to allow their justice. The turn of your countenance I shall never forget, as you said/
ELIZABETH. Oh! do not repeat what I said then. I am most heartily ashamed of it.
MR. DARCY. As a child I was taught what was right. I was given good principles, but left to follow them in pride and conceit. Such I was, and such I might still have been

but for you, dearest, loveliest Elizabeth! By you, I was properly humbled.

(During the song, the ensemble form happy couples while Mr. Darcy speaks with Mr. Bennet. Mrs Bennet looks on, dazed, looking from Mr. Darcy to Elizabeth in complete bewilderment.)

ENSEMBLE.

> NEVER MORE MY LOVE SHALL LEAVE ME!
> NEVER NEVER PART, NO, NEVER MORE!
> LA LA LA LA LA LA LA LA LA LA
> NEVER NEVER PART, NO, NEVER MORE!
> NEVER NEVER PART, NO, NEVER MORE!
> NEVER NEVER PART, NO, NEVER MORE!

(Mr. Bennet agrees to Mr. Darcy's proposal of marriage. Mr. Darcy exits. Jane and Mr. Bennet join Elizabeth.)

SCENE TWELVE

MR. BENNET. Lizzy! Are you out of your senses? Have not you always hated him? He is rich but/

JANE. Oh, Lizzy! It cannot be. I know how much you dislike him/

MR. BENNET. My child, let me not have the grief of seeing you unable to respect your partner in life.

ELIZABETH. This is a wretched beginning, indeed! Have you any other objection, than your belief of my indifference to him?

MR. BENNET. None at all. He is a proud sort of man; but this would be nothing if you really liked him.

ELIZABETH. I do, I do like him. I love him. Indeed he has no improper pride. He is perfectly amiable.

MR. BENNET. Well, if this be the case, he deserves you. I could not have parted with you, my Lizzy, to anyone less worthy. If any young men come for Mary or Kitty, send them in, for I am quite at leisure. *(He exits.)*

JANE. Lizzy. I want to talk very seriously. Will you tell me how long you have loved him?

ELIZABETH. It has been coming on so gradually, that I hardly know when it began; but I believe I must date it from my first seeing his beautiful grounds at Pemberley. *(She laughs.)*

JANE. My dearest sister, now be, be serious!

MRS. BENNET. *(Finally conscious what has happened.)* Good gracious! Mr. Darcy!? And is it really true? Oh, my sweetest Lizzy! How rich and how great you will be! What jewels, what carriages you will have! Jane's is nothing to it — nothing at all. I am so pleased —so happy. Such a charming man! So handsome! So tall! Oh, my dear Lizzy! Three daughters married! Ten thousand a year!

SCENE THIRTEEN

Mr. Darcy sits close to Lizzy as she writes to Longbourn.

ELIZABETH. Why did you look as if you did not care about me?

MR. DARCY. You gave me no encouragement.

ELIZABETH. I was embarrassed.

MR. DARCY. And so was I.

ELIZABETH. You might have talked to me more when you came to the house.

MR. DARCY. A man who had felt less, might.

ELIZABETH. When did these feelings begin?

MR. DARCY. I cannot fix on the hour, or the spot, or the look, or the words...I was in the middle of them before I knew they had begun.

(He steals kisses between her words which she speaks aloud as she writes.)

ELIZABETH. "We will go round the Park every day. I am the happiest creature in the world. Darcy sends his love."

MR. DARCY. *(Kissing her.)* Not all of it.

(The letter falls as they embrace. Mrs. Bennet picks it up.)

MRS. BENNET. *(Reading.)* "You are all welcome to Pemberley at Christmas. Yours, Mrs. Darcy."

EPILOGUE

The cast gathers to sing BEGONE DULL CARE.

ENSEMBLE.
    BEGONE! DULL CARE
    I PRITHEE, BE GONE FROM ME
    BEGONE! DULL CARE
    YOU AND I SHALL NEVER AGREE.

LONG TIME HAST THOU
BEEN TARRYING HERE
AND FAIN THOU WOULDST ME KILL
BUT I' FAITH, DULL CARE
THOU NEVER SHALL HAVE THY WILL.

TOO MUCH CARE
WILL MAKE A YOUNG MAN TURN GREY
AND TOO MUCH CARE
WILL TURN AN OLD MAN TO CLAY.
MY WIFE SHALL DANCE AND I WILL SING
SO MERRILY PASS THE DAY

FOR I HOLD IT ONE OF THE WISEST THINGS
TO DRIVE DULL CARE AWAY
FOR I HOLD IT ONE OF THE WISEST THINGS
TO DRIVE DULL CARE AWAY.

OF PLAY.